LIAM BECKETT was born in Ballymoney, County Antrim. A plumber by trade, he played football for Crusaders and Coleraine in the Irish League, as well as for Drogheda in the League of Ireland, before moving into management. In 1988 he became Robert Dunlop's mechanic, manager and mentor, a partnership that ended only with Dunlop's tragic death at the North West 200 in 2008. Beckett is a sports pundit on BBC Radio Ulster and writes a weekly football column for the *Sunday Life*. He is involved with a number of local charities, and is a patron of both the Harry Gregg Foundation and the Compass Advocacy Network, and an ambassador for the Samaritans. In 2017 he was awarded an MBE for services to sport and to the voluntary sector in Northern Ireland.

LIAM BECKETT
OLD SCHOOL

BECKETT, BIKES,
BALLS & ALL

·THE·
BLACK
·STAFF·
PRESS

For my big brother Lawrence,
who always had my back when
I was growing up.

First published in 2019 by Blackstaff Press
an imprint of Colourpoint Creative Ltd, Colourpoint House,
Jubilee Business Park, 21 Jubilee Road,
Newtownards, BT23 4YH

Printed in Berwick-upon-Tweed by Martins the Printers

A CIP catalogue for this book is available from the British Library

ISBN 978-1-78073-235-0

www.blackstaffpress.com

Follow Liam on Twitter: @liam_beckett

CONTENTS

Foreword

In football and in life the easiest thing to do is not to have an opinion, to sit on the fence and not to say what you think. I don't have a problem with people who choose to be that way – each to their own. What I will say, though, is that I admire people who choose to put their head above the parapet. It won't make them popular but they still decide to say, 'Here, wait a minute. I don't agree.'

Liam has always been my type of man, always has been since we first met many years ago. He doesn't just give an opinion, but when asked Beckett says it exactly how it is, which more often than not doesn't please the do-gooders.

I enjoy Liam's company. We spend our time talking, being very honest with each other. We don't always agree but, in my eyes, that is the way it should be.

The Liam Beckett I have known for many years is not the radio and television presenter or the newspaper columnist, it's the Liam Beckett brought up on football at the cricket park in Ballymoney. Never mind the charity work and all the nice words. There is no doubt in my mind that if you had a problem, you would want Liam on your side.

Liam, we all know, is a good lad. But for me, he is a great friend.

Harry Gregg

Preface

If someone had told me that one day I would write a book, I would have thought they were crazy. That's not what someone from my background would ever have thought about doing. And yet here I am, having just finished my second book. Like most things in my life, it's sport that's taken me down this road. As a youngster, football was my life and I was lucky enough to make a career in the sport, first as a player and then as a manager. Road racing has also been a great passion of mine and I spent twenty of the best years of my life working closely with the late great road racing king, Robert Dunlop. My football and road racing careers opened other doors for me in later life – my newspaper column and my commentary work for the BBC have kept me very much involved in the sports that I love.

When I wrote my first book, *Full Throttle*, in 2016, I wanted to pay tribute to Robert and to our road racing years together. I thought that was it for me as far as books went but, as time has gone on, I've realised that I have more to say about sport, especially football, and about how it shaped me. I wasn't born into a family with money, and education wasn't for me – it's sport that has given me all the chances and opportunities I've had in life. There are plenty of laughs and great stories in this book – and you won't be surprised that I get a few things off my chest too – but hopefully there's plenty to inspire you and to remind you that sport can transform people's lives. That's what life has taught me. I hope you get the message.

PART ONE BIKES

My road racing journey

So much of my life has revolved around road racing, and I've had an incredible journey. One minute I was a young lad poking my head through a hedge to watch my heroes race and the next I was wheeling Robert Dunlop's bike on to the grid at world-famous circuits, working with him as he claimed victory after victory.

Being from the small town of Ballymoney in north Antrim, I was always aware of road racing. The North West 200 took place just a stone's throw from where I grew up. I went fairly regularly on Sunday-school trips to Portstewart and Portrush 'to see the sea' but it wasn't until I was eight that I saw my first road race. My big brother, Lawrence, and some of his mates decided to walk the twelve miles from my grandmother's house in Balnamore to the North West circuit, leaving early in the morning. I was armed with a brown paper bag of tomato sandwiches and kitted out in a pair of worn-out gutties. It was never going to end well, and it turned out to be a journey I would never wish to repeat or inflict on my worst enemy. Lawrence and his pals kept telling me that the race was just over the next hill. They told me that for about six miles. But there was no sign of the sea. I was so tired.

When we finally arrived, the race had already started and the only vantage point left was the roof of the public toilets, which were on the approach into Portstewart. We scrambled up there and watched the bikes flying down to the harbour. The smell of two-stroke was everywhere and the sensation of speed was incredible. I was smitten. I have no memory of how we got home but I do remember feeling that I had had a brilliant experience, even though I had blistered feet and had discovered on arrival that my tomato sandwiches had fallen out of the arse of my sodden brown paper bag.

I got to know a lot more about road racing when I met Jackie Graham, who was Joey Dunlop's mechanic – a man who was well and truly hooked on the sport. He was courting my aunt Sally, my mum's sister, and he and Sally used to come to my mum's house to visit frequently. Jackie used to take me out on the back of his Triumph Bonneville. I would have been about twelve then, and he scared the shit out of me as we sped around. My mum was always telling him not to go so fast but once we were out of her sight, he went like the clappers. It was scary and exhilarating – and gave me an early insight into why people race and the buzz they get.

Jackie was a genius with machinery – the most gifted mechanical engineer I have ever met. He was a foreman fitter at Corfield's camera factory in Ballymoney, fixing the cameras when they broke. In his spare time he loved working on bikes. Eventually, he left Corfield's and, after a stint at Sherwood Medical Industries as a machine setter engineer, he set up his own motorcycle tuning and repair business, and started working as a mechanic, fettling Joey's bikes in his spare time. Jackie's mum, Martha, and Joey's dad, Willie, were brother and sister, so the boys were full cousins, and they had the utmost respect for each other.

I formed a very strong bond with Jackie, one that I still have to this day. My father had died when I was two and Jackie became a kind of father figure to me – as well as the runs on the bike, he'd take me fishing (illegally, more often

4

than not). We used to wade through the river in the dark, the water chest-high, Jackie poking the bank to disturb the fish while I 'ginnled' them with a wire mesh net. We never failed to catch a few.

When I was a teenager, football was my first love but the bikes were a close second. I had divided loyalties – sometimes I'd be playing in an Irish League game and I'd be thinking about the road race that was being run that day. One half of me wanted to go to the football and the other half wanted to go to the race. Initially I made my career in football, but the bikes got me in the end. In the latter part of my playing career, I was suffering with a groin injury and couldn't play for long without constant pain, and that made the pull of the bikes even stronger.

I had always known the Dunlops, of course. I had gone to school with Joey – he used to talk to me about football and I used to talk to him about the bikes. Later, Joey's success on the bikes meant that everyone knew him. I was also aware of up-and-coming Robert. I remember seeing him at the Mid-Antrim and being impressed. Joey by that stage was a star, making headlines and setting records, but Robert was a real talent too. In 1988, Jackie told me Robert was struggling for space to work on his bikes, and that's when I offered him my workshop. Fairly soon, I started working with Robert part time and then pretty much full time as his mechanic and mentor – we went everywhere together.

Robert and I ended up working together for over twenty years. We were a small outfit and that suited us just fine. Very quickly, we bonded – we had a similar sense of humour – and that bond became deeper as we got to know one another. There was trust and respect between us.

He knew that I would do anything to help him and I knew that he would do anything he could to fulfil the faith I had in him. He became the younger brother I never had. Most of the time it was just the two of us, heads down, at the bikes. We were often on the road and, during those twenty years, we did all the major road races in Northern Ireland and all of the smaller races across the island, as well as the Isle of Man TT multiple times. We also travelled to places like Mettet in Belgium and as far as Macau in southern China to race.

Now and again, Robert and I got to travel in style to races but most of the time we used whatever mode of transport was the cheapest. We sometimes went by boat to the Isle of Man TT but more often than not we took small, private planes – kites, we used to call them – from Newtownards or Aghadowey airstrips. And we had one particularly memorable trip from the City of Derry airport.

A man I knew had a small three-seater plane and he offered to fly Robert and me to the island for a keen price. However, on the day we were due to depart, the weather was awful – gale-force winds and torrential rain. It was so bad that I got in touch with the pilot to check if the flight was going ahead. To my surprise, he said he was still happy to take the plane up. Robert's brother Jim drove us from Ballymoney to the airport and the weather was so bad that even he said that nobody in their right mind would go up in a wee plane on a day like that.

When we arrived, the pilot was waiting for us in reception and confirmed that we were flying. If I was in a similar situation now, I wouldn't dream of taking that flight, but I was a lot younger back then and so was Robert. I wasn't surprised that Robert was happy to fly, though – he was much more of a daredevil than me and nothing fazed him. In fact, I often felt the greater the challenge or the greater the risk, the more Robert relished it.

On the runway was what seemed to me the smallest aeroplane ever built, with just two tiny seats in the back and one at the front for the pilot. It was so small that it was something of an ordeal to even get inside the bloody thing, but eventually all three of us clambered in and got settled – the pilot was practically sitting on our knees. Even on the tarmac, the wee plane was being quite badly buffeted by the wind and rain, but soon we were hurtling up the runway and were airborne. We couldn't have been more than fifty feet up when we were completely engulfed in cloud. It was like being wrapped in cotton wool – but not in a good way. The plane was tiny and our faces were practically jammed against the windows as the cloud pressed in on us. I genuinely feared for my life.

I kept telling myself that the pilot knew what he was doing and that I had to trust him – but I was also concerned that there was a considerable amount of rain leaking in through the pilot's door and that the floor of the plane was getting very wet. During the flight, which felt like a roller-coaster ride, I could clearly see that the pilot, who was a lovely man, was sweating profusely. I suspected he knew it had been a mistake to take the plane up.

Despite the horrendous flying conditions and me being filled to the throat with the fear of God, any time I glanced over at Robert he was smiling. He was either completely fearless or he was trying his damnedest to alleviate my fears – my guess is a combination of both. It seemed like an eternity but at last the pilot told us we were over the Isle of Man (I could have kissed him), and that he was about to begin his descent towards Ronaldsway airport. As we descended from the extremely low cloud, however, we saw that we were, in fact, over the Calf of Man, which is nowhere near the airport. The pilot had seriously miscalculated and had to quickly pull us back up again, only just clearing the trees and other obstacles around us. A few minutes later he took us down again and this time when we emerged from the clouds we were over the airport and, barring the odd bump, hop, and skip, he landed the plane safely.

It felt good to be alive and in one piece. Even Robert looked pale. There wasn't much chat during the half-hour car journey from the airport to the island capital Douglas, where we were always based. We all rode our luck that day and, although it was a terrifying experience, it was one of those moments that I shared with Robert and I treasure it for that.

Those years with Robert were a roller-coaster time, and my 2017 book, *Full Throttle: Robert Dunlop, Road Racing and Me*, tells that story in detail. The highs were plenty because of Robert's talent. He won so many major international races – the NW 200, Isle of Man TT, Ulster Grand Prix, British Championship and Macau Grand Prix – but when he had a crash, it was generally always a big one, and when he fell off, he always seemed to hit something hard. If there was a pole on a mile-long road, you could be sure that Robert would hit it. And yet I could count on the fingers of one hand the number of times he fell off due to rider error. Those crashes never dented his confidence, though the '94 crash at the Isle of Man TT, when his rear wheel broke up, virtually finished him in terms of racing any machinery above 125cc class. His career had been headed towards World Superbikes, but the crash put an end to that.

Together, Robert and I experienced some very public lows in the sport – some awful accidents and the loss of fellow riders and, especially in the early days, the real struggle to get sponsorship. I always felt that Robert didn't get the investment he deserved. I remember one occasion when Joey had to pull out of a race and we were hopeful that Robert might get his allocation of Michelin tyres. It didn't work out in the end – we were refused. We had the last laugh, though, because Robert went on to win the race anyway. Which was almost always the story for us – the lows were more than compensated for by the highs. A real highlight was when Robert became British champion in 1991, winning every race bar one (even though he crossed the finish line in first place). He became a regular winner against the world's best at the major international events, and no event was more memorable than his win at the Macau Grand Prix in 1989. We were so chuffed to see the Dunlop name on one of the few trophies that didn't already have it.

Robert was such a bright talent when I started working with him, full of potential. I'd like to think I brought him more focus and self-belief. It became clear to me that although his ability was never in question, he did lack confidence – in part because he was so much in awe of big brother Joey. It was my job to convince him that he didn't have to be another Joey. In fact, I made it clear that there never would be another Joey. He needed to concentrate on being Robert Dunlop, a star in his own right. It filled me with pride and a great sense of achievement to see Robert realise his potential and become a global star. His dreams came true and so did mine. Working with him took me inside the world of road racing in a way that I'd only dreamed of. This was a sport that I loved but had only ever watched from behind a hedge. Now I was fortunate to be part of the story of the Dunlops, the greatest road racing family in the world.

As time went on, the Dunlops became like a second family to me. I would have been around at Robert's parents' house at least once a week – Robert adored his mum and dad, so we were there regularly. And it was like any other house out in the country – as soon as you arrived the kettle would go on. I suppose they were my kind of people. They hadn't started out with lots of resources or money but they had made good. Robert and Joey had tremendous racing ability but they also were grafters and absolutely dedicated.

The boys' father, William – they called him Willie Da – was also a tremendously talented mechanic. He was always hands-on with the boys and he was absolutely even-handed; 50 per cent of his time went to Robert and 50 per cent went to Joey. The whole family was a great source of support for Joey and Robert. They didn't always go to the races but they were always behind the boys. Brother Jim was similar to Willie Da, and gave a lot of his time to Joey and Robert, again dividing his time equally. There were no favourites.

They were a very close family. Jim and Willie went to the races and tried to share their time equally between both boys. The women of the family rarely went to the races. Quite often, the women would have got together at one of their houses around race time. I think it was to keep one another company and maybe to give a bit of support to each another. They weren't interested in spats or being critical of other riders. It wasn't in their nature to badmouth other people. I always admired them for that.

I know that Robert's mother, May, counted on me as someone who would always tell her the truth, even when it meant telling her something she wouldn't want to hear. In 1994, when Robert had his awful crash at the TT, May was getting conflicting reports about his condition. It was bloody hard but I told her what was actually happening – that Robert was in a very bad way. She later told me that she really respected me for that. We've all been through a lot together – good and bad. I feel quite protective of the family and they know I have their back.

It was shortly after Robert's death in 2008 that I received a call from Ballymoney Borough Council asking if I could call in to see the chief executive about their plan to create a permanent memorial for Robert in his hometown of Ballymoney. The council had already created a beautiful memorial garden for Joey at the lower end of the town and they wanted to create something similar for Robert, who they quite rightly felt had also been a tremendous ambassador for the borough. The chief executive suggested three different locations for consideration, one of which was directly adjacent to Joey's garden.

I acted as the liaison between the council and Robert's family – his wife, Louise, his sons and his mum, May. We decided that the proposed site beside Joey was the one and only place to commemorate Robert. The council was prepared to fund the entire construction and maintenance of Robert's memorial garden, just as they had for Joey's.

However, we also felt that there ought to be a bronze sculpture of Robert, just as there was of Joey. Joey's statue had been funded by Honda and an anonymous sponsor. We were confident that we could raise the money for Robert's statue from voluntary public donations. We set up a small fundraising committee consisting of Robert's family and my family plus a family friend called Sammy McClements and identified a sculptor from Scotland called David Annand who specialises in sports sculptures. David gave us a quotation in excess of £40,000, which was obviously an enormous amount of money, but which we also felt was reasonable, given the quality of his work and the scale of the piece. And so began the mammoth task of raising the money.

Hundreds of people donated and helped to raise money and within a year we were able to commission the statue. The pose was chosen by Robert's wife Louise and it's iconic – Robert is standing on the top step of the podium raising a bottle of champagne in the air in celebration of yet another of his famous victories. I thought Louise's choice summed Robert up perfectly and the statue was everything we could have hoped for. Together, the memorials to Robert and Joey are called the Dunlop Memorial Gardens and they attract thousands of visitors every year. They are a space for everyone to pay tribute to two legends of the sport.

I remember Robert especially when I am at the NW200, the race at which he tragically died in 2008, but until July 2015 I hadn't had the opportunity to visit the memorial that stands at the scene of Joey's fatal accident at the Tallinn road race in Estonia. Crusaders Football Club had just won the 2015 Irish League Championship, which then enabled them to take their place in the first qualifying round of the European Champions League, and as fate would have it they were drawn against Levadia Tallinn from Estonia. BBC Sport NI offered me the opportunity to cover the game for *Sportsound*, so I agreed to travel over with my long-time mate and fellow commentator, Joel Taggart.

As soon as I knew I was going to Tallinn, I started to make plans to visit Joey's memorial on the outskirts of the city. Our trip coincided with the anniversary of Joey's death on 2 July, so it seemed a particularly fitting time to pay my respects. Due to work commitments, we ended up going to the memorial on 6 July. Joel came with me and I was glad of the company. I'd never been to the memorial before and I knew it would be a sad occasion.

Tallinn FC had laid on a driver to take us to the memorial. That morning, before we went, we headed downtown and bought the loveliest bunch of yellow flowers – they were a perfect match for the colour of Joey's helmet. I also had a special handmade card, laminated to make it weatherproof, that was signed by Joey's mum, sisters and brother, Jim, and that they had given me to leave at the memorial. The family also asked me to leave flowers on their behalf. Only Jim and Robert had been to the memorial before – the rest of the family hadn't had the opportunity to visit, so it meant a lot to them that I was going.

The memorial is at the exact spot on the Pirita-Kose-Kloostrimetsa track where Joey lost his life. I got the driver who had brought us there to take us on a full lap of the circuit. I suppose I wanted to walk a bit in Joey's footsteps. I was immediately struck by how dangerous the track was, with many heavily forested areas right beside it. Joey's memorial was in one of those areas. It's very simple, just a raised mound with a plaque on it. However, there were lots of tributes and messages – people had even left shirts with messages on them pinned to the trees. It was very moving and quite surreal. I walked down the road, past where the memorial was and walked back, trying to get a sense of what had happened the day that Joey crashed. It did make me sad to be there that day, but I was glad I went. Joey died far from home and it meant a lot to me to see where it had happened and to be there to show my respects in person. It gave me a kind of closure, to be able to see things for myself. And there was comfort in seeing those tributes and messages – to know that Joey is still loved and remembered.

As the 2018 North West 200 came on the horizon, it seemed unbelievable to me that Robert had died at the race ten years before. The family was keen to organise a memorial lap on the circuit in his memory and they asked me to help with the organisation. The memorial lap was a great idea in all kinds of ways. Not only was it a very fitting way to remember Robert but it also became a focus for everyone, the family and me. The anniversary was an emotional time, so it was good to be busy and the arrangements and organisation around the event were a distraction.

It would have been wonderful if we'd been able to arrange the lap for the Friday night, when more people would have been around, but our request was turned down because the circuit is generally gridlocked with traffic and it would have been impossible to stage Robert's memorial lap in a properly controlled and legal fashion. After discussions with the PSNI, it was decided that, for safety reasons, the lap would be held on the Wednesday evening of race week.

The turnout for the lap was incredible. We had expected a couple of hundred bike fans, but thousands turned up on their various types and colours of bikes. They had come from all over Ireland and the UK to pay their respects. It was a fantastic spectacle as they all set off on a silent lap, controlled at the front by outriders from the NW200 Marshals Association. I had a lump in my throat as the stream of riders left the starting point at the Metropole Corner car park. I know that night meant a lot to the family. They wanted to keep Robert's memory alive and that turnout was proof in spades that Robert was not forgotten, that he was still loved and that he still had an important place in the sport.

The event would have been impossible without Cathal Cunning from the NW200 Marshals Association, who supplied several personnel to enable us to stage the lap safely, and the PSNI, who provided officers to manage all road junctions and to assist with traffic.

Robert's memorial lap had two purposes – to remember Robert and to raise money for the Injured Riders' Welfare Fund, the charity chosen by Robert's family. Established in 2003, the fund aims to help riders after injury by providing support and financial assistance to them and their families. Each rider who participated in the tribute lap made a donation. Robert's mum, May; his sisters Margaret, Helen and Linda; his brother, Jim; and his wife, Louise, were all there, and presented each rider with a memorial lap certificate. The family also commissioned special commemorative badges that were sold on the night, with those proceeds going to the Air Ambulance Northern Ireland.

Although I'm not hands-on now, in terms of working

with a specific rider, I still attend all the major road races as a commentator for the BBC. I've been commentating for about ten years now and it's a job that I enjoy. It keeps me in touch with the sport but it also gives me a different perspective. When I worked with Robert, I was at the heart of the action, in the thick of it in the workshop and in the pit lane. During the races I could only guess at what was going on around the circuit and, barring accidents, what was happening elsewhere only mattered to me if it impacted on Robert. Of course I wanted an incident-free race but his safety was my top priority, with the result a close second. We used to say that second place is really only the first loser.

I would have been very apprehensive and very uptight on the day of a race, although I would have been doing my best to hide that from Robert as it was me who was meant to be giving him confidence. En route to many of the races, particularly the majors, I would have had a knot in my stomach. Now, I have a much more relaxed life as a commentator. Instead of feeling responsible for Robert's welfare and worrying about the reliability of the machinery, my main concern now is minding my Ps and Qs on air.

Of course, the twenty years that I spent with Robert are a tremendous help to me in the commentary box. They gave me a real sense of what it's like to prepare for a race, what it's like in the van and in the paddock. I understand how riders analyse all the various elements of a race – corners, machinery, tyre compounds, weather conditions, etc. – and hopefully that means I can give the listeners a better insight into what's going on in the minds of the riders. I have a different perspective these days –

both because I am no longer entirely fixated on one rider, and also because of the technical advances that enable us to follow almost every moment of the race. Innovations like static, machine- and kerb-mounted cameras, as well as eye-in-the-sky helicopters, provide spectacular viewing for fans in their living rooms – and make the jobs of the commentators much easier, and more exciting.

Despite all my years of involvement in the sport and experience, the very mention of a red flag – this is used when a race is stopped because of an emergency – in my earpiece still sends a shiver up my spine. Of course, a red flag can sometimes be used when there is debris on the track or when a minor accident has dislodged safety bales and the organisers must put them all back. However, a red flag can also indicate an incident of a serious nature and on some occasions these incidents involve the death of a rider. A fatal incident is the worst possible news and very difficult to handle. Having spent over thirty years in the sport I have trained myself to stay calm and I always try to remain optimistic. The BBC producer, via the clerk of the course, will usually very quickly forward us the information about how serious the incident is and, of course, we are well aware of the need to play down an incident and most definitely not mention the name of the rider or riders involved until we are completely sure that we have permission from the clerk of the course to do so.

When we are made aware that someone has died it's very difficult not to let that affect the commentary. Until we know for definite what has happened, we avoid talking about the incident on air but, of course, it's still in the back of your mind and, unknowingly, that can come through in the commentary. I've had people tell me that they suspected that the news wasn't good simply by the tone of my voice, and I can understand how that happens. We're only human and it's virtually impossible to sound jovial or enthusiastic when you've just been fed the news that a competitor has been killed. All of us in the commentary studio just want to pack up and go home. The days when riders are seriously injured or killed are tough indeed.

Despite many facets of the sport having changed over the years, and in spite of my own move from the pit lane to the commentary box, the one thing that has never changed for me is the immense admiration I have for the competitors, organisers and volunteers involved in road racing. Commentating means that I still feel part of the road racing family – and I definitely have more of a connection with the fans. In the old days, I only spoke to a handful of fans, the ones that were in the pit lane or paddock. Now I get to talk to thousands. I'll never forget the intensity and buzz of those years with Robert, but I feel so lucky that I'm still so involved in the sport that I love.

Road

For me, the most compelling film ever produced on road racing is *Road* (2014). This documentary was the brainchild of Dermot Lavery and Michael Hewitt, the two principals of Belfast-based DoubleBand films. It's a brilliant and sensitive production, and I still find it heartbreaking every time I see it.

Narrated by Liam Neeson, *Road* tells the story of two generations of the Dunlop family – brothers Joey and

Robert, and Robert's sons, Michael and William. The Dunlops are road racing royalty and the film is a celebration of that fact. However, it also captures the deep vein of tragedy that runs through the Dunlop story and the impact on the family of the deaths of Joey and Robert.

Road racing and the Dunlop name go hand in hand. The family epitomises the very heart and soul of road racing. There isn't any other family that has given so much and lost so much to the sport, yet still continues to participate. The Dunlops were for DoubleBand a compelling and natural focus for a documentary on road racing. The irony is that they are such a humble, modest family, uncomfortable and uneasy with the stardom and publicity that the sport has brought them. They've always preferred to remain under the radar. The fact that the family agreed to be involved in the production is a testament to the care that DoubleBand took to create something authentic and true.

I knew DoubleBand from way back. Robert and I had worked with Dermot and Michael in the early nineties on a DoubleBand production called *Between the Hedges*, which was filmed during the 1992 racing season in Northern Ireland and featured Robert. They did a good job with that and I always thought that they were sensitive and very professional. They called me up in 2010 and asked me if I'd work with them as a consultant on a documentary they wanted to make about the Dunlops. The result would be *Road*. Over the next four years, I met regularly with Michael and Dermot to help coordinate things with the Dunlop family and to advise them on various aspects of the film. For example, I'd be one of the few people left who would have known the kinds of conversations that

Robert and Joey would have had in the garage.

The documentary team spent months attending road racing meetings, including the international events such as the NW 200, the Ulster Grand Prix and the Isle of Man TT, together with many of the smaller national meetings. They shot hours and hours of live-action races as well as conducting interviews with the Dunlop family and with members of the road racing family. In the documentary, the live action footage is cut with interviews and with commentary by Liam Neeson. The entire production was methodically planned. The Dunlop family and the other contributors were given ample time to collect their thoughts. There's never a sense that the production is attempting to sensationalise the storyline. There was no need to – the fact is that the Dunlop story would be almost unbelievable if it wasn't true.

DoubleBand conducted some interviews at people's homes but some were carried out at a specially set-up studio at the Lodge Hotel in Coleraine. That's where my interview was shot. They did a great job of editing my section because I completely choked up and was in tears a few times during filming. But I was always encouraged to take a five-minute break and a glass of water and compose myself. When I began to talk about my memories, particularly of Robert, I struggled to hold back the tears. He was like the kid brother I never had. I loved him dearly and I still miss him big time. I know how much he loved his family and I know how much he loved road racing and for him to be taken from us at such a young age is still hard to stomach. Participating in *Road* brought a lot of those feelings flooding back.

I can remember attending DoubleBand headquarters in Belfast to view an almost-complete version of the film. I was only minutes in when big tears were falling down my face. In fairness, Dermot and Michael had offered me a pack of paper hankies before they turned down the lights in the studio but I had laughed the suggestion off, thinking I was a big hard lad. I was wrong. The documentary did bring back some great memories but it brought a lot of sadness too. It's those one-on-one interviews with the family that hit me hardest – watching Joey and Robert's mother, May; Joey and Robert's sister Linda; and Robert's sons William and Michael, struggling with raw emotion and grief is a heartbreaking watch. Even pretty hardened non-family members, like Barry Symmons, ex-Honda team boss, are visibly upset trying to give their individual and personal accounts of their memories and recollections of the Dunlops.

Road ambushed me in a way I didn't expect. I knew the facts of the Dunlop story and I thought I had pretty much made my peace with all of it, so I wasn't prepared for the way that the film made the loss and grief real for me again. It was surreal hearing Joey and Robert being talked about in the past tense, and it was heartbreaking hearing the family talking so openly and honestly about the deaths of Joey and Robert. I was with the family a lot when Robert died and we comforted and supported one another. But a lot of that comfort and support was unspoken – a hug, a hand on your shoulder, shared tears. I'd never heard the family speak about their loss, and it was so raw and emotional, more so because each person spoke directly to camera and was alone on screen. The personal price this family had paid was beyond words and far outweighed any race triumph or any sense of celebration. It was unbearable. I'm not sure what it would be like to watch it now, with William gone too.

Several premieres were planned for *Road*, the first being at the Movie House cinema on the Dublin Road in Belfast. It was a packed house, with a magnificent one-million-pound sound system amplifying the sound of motorbikes around the theatre. Lots of media people and celebrities were present and I've yet to meet one who wasn't in tears during some part of the film, even some of my more hardened colleagues! DoubleBand had delegated a fella to look after my every need that evening. And by God, he did. Just prior to the curtain going up he'd asked me if I wanted or needed anything. I said I wouldn't mind a bottle of beer, and off he went. Little did I know when I made this requesst that he'd have to leave the building and run up the street to the nearest bar to get me a beer, and then rush back to the cinema and across the seats to present me with it.

There was also a premiere in London's Leicester Square, and Michael and William Dunlop and I were flown over for three days. On the day of the premiere, I took a walk up to the cinema where the film was to be screened. A red carpet was being rolled out and crowd barriers were being erected. I said to one of the guys erecting the barriers, 'Are you expecting a big crowd?' to which he replied, 'Yes, we are, mate. Rumour has it Liam might be coming.' Don't laugh, but for a split second I stopped and thought, 'Holy shit, I knew a few people had heard of me in Ballymoney …' until the penny dropped and I realised he was talking about Liam Neeson.

That night I met Suzi Perry, who was hosting the premiere, and she told me that she'd heard that the cinema had considered using subtitles because of the strong North Antrim accents in the film. Thankfully, they had decided to run it as it was. During the premiere that night I sat beside a burly man who shook my hand when I took my seat and informed me he was a film critic. The big man cried his eyes out throughout the documentary and when the lights went on at the end, he was so apologetic for crying. I told him not to be concerned in the slightest because everyone cried when they watched this film. He was a cockney and I asked him if he'd understood our accents, to which he replied, 'Yes, Liam, I understood every word,' so that was good enough for me.

Not surprisingly, *Road* went on to huge success and critical acclaim. It brought more fans to the sport because, for the first time, it gave a proper insight into the dangers and the heartbreak and skill involved in road racing. Often, the sport is in the news for negative reasons and that really colours people's perceptions of it. It's this kind of news that the critics and sceptics seize on. What was so important about *Road* was that it gave audiences a more complete sense of the whole of that world and of the real people involved, through the story of an ordinary working-class family. It gave a personal dimension to heartbreak and success, and the urge to compete. It was a game-changer.

The road racing family

The world of road racing has always felt like home to me. Maybe that's because road racing is, by and large, a working-class sport and I am more comfortable in working-class company. It's the kind of environment I grew up in and know. By and large, the people involved in road racing are not false and, while the world of road racing is less wealthy than other forms of motorsport, there is a solid core of genuine warmth and honesty that some other sports, such as Formula 1, lack. And although golf is far more accessible to people now – I love a game of golf – there are still some stuffy clubs where it's all about money and contacts. Don't misunderstand me, I'd like to see more prize money for the riders in road racing. Compared to what sportspeople involved in professional golf and professional football earn, road racers are, by far, the poor relations, and riders ought to be properly rewarded for the risks they take.

What I love about road racing is that no one looks down their nose at anyone else and the riders are not full of their own importance. I absolutely detest snobbery and bad manners (and they usually come together). In general, what wealthy people have they hold whereas with the road racing family, what they have they share. They've got bigger hearts and they are more genuine. It's no secret either that many road racing critics and sceptics are from middle- or upper-class backgrounds and it's my sense that this also plays a part in their criticism of the sport and its people.

I remember in the early days, if you needed a loan of a piece of tape or a pair of pliers before a race, you didn't run to the paddock or to your van, you just went to the first van you came to and you helped yourself. Sometimes Robert and I would come back to our van to find a rider or a mechanic returning a screwdriver or something else they'd borrowed. Fans could just walk up to the back of Robert's or Joey's vans and watch as we worked on and prepared the bikes. And they could walk through the paddock and see all the big names and all the wee names side by side – all at the backs of their vans, fettling their bikes. Some of the biggest riders sometimes had a wee rope around their bikes, just for a bit of space, but it wouldn't have blocked anyone's view or access. That's the way it was – fans and riders together. It was all part of a fantastic era for the sport.

However, I could see changes coming into the sport in the nineties. Instead of riders arriving at a race in old T-shirts and jackets, more and more of them were turning up in shirts embroidered with team and sponsors' logos. A small thing – but it was followed by other kinds of branding, and suddenly all of those small things combined and led to what I realise now was a major change in the sport – the introduction of giant awnings and grandstands at the major races. Back in the day you might have come across someone with a bit of money who had a small awning, but most of us just threw plastic sheets over the bikes and our other bits and pieces. Now, a lot of the top teams have awnings big enough to house not just the bikes but also tables and chairs. The sad fact is that, a lot of the time, these awnings are completely zipped up, meaning that the top riders are removed from the fans and have much less personal interaction with them. You don't see some of the riders until five minutes before the race. In the past, riders were very much in the mix with the fans, members of the family, but the increased distance between the stars of the sport and their supporters means we're losing part of what has given road racing its identity. The sport is the poorer for it, in my opinion.

We all know that road racing is high risk, and that the riders need their own time, space and privacy. They can't be expected to be always signing autographs and having photos taken. But there is a middle ground. Many people have said to me that they feel that top stars are being kept away from the fans and wrapped in cotton wool. It certainly does feel that team bosses are creating an environment that enables certain riders to stay isolated. Fans need to be able to meet their heroes. It's part of the lifeblood of the sport. I'm of the opinion that designated meet-the-rider sessions at races – which would give fans a chance to get pictures and autographs – might be one way of making this happen. We are a family and that is the spirit of the sport, the heartbeat of the sport, and we must ensure we never lose that. God forbid that we ever go down the road of Formula 1 and end up in a them-and-us scenario.

In the old days, too, people were packed in around hedges and around the roads but access to lots of the areas where you used to be able to spectate is now prohibited. Many fans can no longer get really close to the course and are concentrated in large grandstands, for example at the North West. Fans are kept at a distance from the sport by health and safety regulations. It's a bitter pill to swallow – maybe not so much for the younger generation but certainly for old stagers like me.

Road racing has, of course, become much more professional and there's more money in the sport now – at least for some. But it's still only the very top riders who can call themselves professionals, and who can earn a decent living from the sport. Such is the expense of competing for privateers and small teams that very often the prize money, if they are fortunate enough to win, comes nowhere near to covering the cost of competing.

Races such as Armoy, Cookstown and Tandragee – the smaller national road races – still retain that old-school identity and atmosphere that is missing from bigger events. At these races, you can still take a walk through the paddock and smell a frying pan in full flight – the way road racing used to be at every circuit. And I think that's why these events are still so popular. The bigger international meetings have become much more corporate and are run more like businesses. I suppose that's how it has to be but I don't want to lose what initially made me fall in love with road racing – that it was honest-to-goodness, happy-go-lucky, open and transparent. Gone are the days when you used to get a shout to come into a competitor's van for a cup of tea and, if you were in luck, a slice of toast – you had to check for mould, of course. That rarely happens any more.

There have been other damaging losses too. The Dundrod 150, Killinchy 150, Temple 100, Mid Antrim 150, Monaghan, Carrowdore 100, Sligo 100, Athea, Fore, Kells, Faugheen and Dundalk races are just some of the small national events that acted as a training ground for the riders of Robert and Joey's generation. They are all gone now and their disappearance has been extremely detrimental to young up-and-coming road racers. We all have a responsibility to help these young riders serve a proper apprenticeship. Many are now arriving at the three majors – the Isle of Man TT, Ulster Grand Prix and North West 200 – without the valuable experience that comes from participation in smaller road races. I believe that they are being catapulted on to the big scene too soon. A lot of young ones end up being touted in the press as potential winners for major international road races without having had the necessary experience and track time. And if top riders are thin on the ground at those races, young riders get pushed up the grid, which sometimes means they put more pressure on themselves.

Although short-circuit racing is very different to road racing, it's the arena in which Joey and Robert, and that whole generation, cut their teeth. It provided them with track time, something that's essential if you're trying to learn how to race a motorcycle at high speed. Robert used to be racing every other week and it served as an important apprenticeship for the sport. Those smaller national races were also a great opportunity to mix with more established riders, to see how they conducted themselves and to get insights into how to cope with the pressures of the sport. Perhaps we need a proper taskforce to be set up, one that will look into getting Aghadowey race track, for example, back up and running, together with sourcing government funding towards upgrading the likes of Nutts Corner, Kirkistown and Bishopscourt, and so on. Providing proper short circuits in Northern Ireland would enable young riders to hone and improve their road racing skills. I can see great value in getting a newcomers' championship going, which would at least give young riders a chance to learn and to test their limits and their own machines' limits – such as judging the angle of lean before a tyre loses traction – in a safer environment before they take on major road races. In the event of an accident at a short circuit, the chances are the rider will get up, dust himself down and go again. This might not always be the outcome if the same accident happens at a pure road race.

Maybe I am fighting a losing battle but if I'm to be dragged into modern-day road racing, let me assure you I will be kicking and screaming on the way. I would ask the road racing family to judge if the sport is in a better place now than it was twenty years ago. Sure, there are better facilities, toilets, tarmacked paddocks and so on, but there are fewer smaller races, which used to be an ideal training ground for up-and-coming riders; less contact between riders and fans; and we're in danger of losing that 'family feeling' that gives the sport its heart.

Despite all the changes, it's a testimony to the road racing family that the fans still turn out in their thousands. And I can't speak highly enough of all the volunteers in the sport. Without them it would be financially impossible to sustain road racing. Whether they're setting up the race circuit, helping with course management or in the paddock, acting as scrutineers, assisting the Fire Authority or on the medical side as part of St John's Ambulance or the MCUI medical team, or wherever, volunteers are one of the main reasons why riders and spectators can just turn up on the day and enjoy the spectacle. What race could operate without trained marshalls who are all volunteers and who give of their time completely free of charge?

The anti-road-racing brigade

I detest it when people who know next to nothing about road racing call for it to be banned. Usually, people like this come forward after there's been a serious incident or a fatality. I take great exception to all those people who unthinkingly peddle the notion that the racers are lunatics. Many of them couldn't tell a cam shaft from a calm day and have never been to a road race in their lives. Some criticise because they've been asked to contribute by a media outlet of some kind and will either get a fee or get some attention. Their complete lack of knowledge on the subject means it's impossible for them to offer a balanced, informed or measured opinion. Several other sports are extremely high risk – show-jumping, eventing, horseracing, mountain climbing, fishing (river and sea), motor car racing, and so on. But, as with road racing, people are free to choose whether or not they participate. Those who compete know only too well the risks involved and it's their right to take part if they wish. They live by the code that those who risk nothing become nothing – that he who dares wins. That does mean that they live on the edge but that's what road racing's all about – being fully alive. Unless you are prepared to properly research the sport and get to know those involved in it, then it's my opinion that you should keep your nose out of it.

If a radio or TV programme asked me to join a discussion on a subject I know nothing about I would refuse – particularly if it was a subject as serious as road racing. Really, no one should agree to be part of a serious debate unless they have the knowledge to back up their point of view. If you want to discuss road racing, get involved – go and see a race, meet the racers, find out about it, meet the road racing family, get insights. Then come back and talk to me about it.

Then and now

Just as it has in almost every sphere of life, health and safety has had a major impact on road racing over the last thirty years. Although many of the new policies and procedures are to be welcomed, there is no doubt that we've lost something in the process. Gone are the days when you could find a hole in a hedge and stick your head through it, or sit on a wall or on a fence right beside the action and just a few feet from the racing, where the sensation of speed and being a few feet from racing motorcycles was absolutely incredible. Nowadays, at most road racing circuits, spectators are being pushed further and further back from the action and many of the most popular vantage-points at road races are now 'prohibited areas'.

Gone too, thankfully, are the days of smoking or using open flames around jerrycans full of fuel in the pit lane or indeed anywhere at a race. These are now high-risk areas. I can well remember in years gone by several people, including Robert's father and Robert himself, smoking away around fuel. We never thought of the danger and, of course, the new rules and regulations are all for our own good. The one race in which the bikes still require refuelling and scheduled pit stops is the Isle of Man TT. There is no chance now of being allowed to stand around chatting and smoking in Gasoline Alley. In the past, the people in the pit lane used to look a bit like a pack of liquorice allsorts, with some people in boiler suits, some in jeans and T-shirts – everyone wearing whatever they liked. Now, pit crews are kitted out in fireproof suits, and the crew member responsible for refuelling duties is required to wear not only a fully zipped-up fireproof suit but also a fireproof balaclava and full-length fireproof gloves.

After losing Robert in 2008, I had no interest in returning to Gasoline Alley. However, in 2018, I accepted an invitation from top road racer Maria Costello to help her to refuel her bike at pit stops. I did enjoy being back. Maria is a top-class competitor and one of the very few women competing in a male-dominated sport. She has tremendous skill, technique and commitment but faces massive challenges in sport and is mostly regarded as an underdog. But I've always been a fan of the underdog and perhaps that's what swung it for me and convinced me to help Maria all I can when I'm available.

It was during the 2018 TT Supertwin race that I found out to my cost just how strictly the new rules in Gasoline Alley are applied. Before and during the race, I took the time to emphasis to the other members of Maria's pit crew the importance of a slick pit stop, reminding them that they are an opportunity to gain a few valuable extra seconds and can even push riders a few places up the leader board. I was emphasising to the other two lads that it was essential to stay calm and collected. It's easy to panic with a massive, packed grandstand looking on. It can be quite intimidating.

It was shortly after Maria had set sail down Glencrutchery Road towards Bray Hill at the very start of the race that the three of us in the crew made our way down to our designated pit in Gasoline Alley. Getting to the pit lane reasonably quickly after your rider has left is important, not only because it takes a bit of time to get accustomed to the atmosphere there, but also so that you are prepared for all eventualities when your rider arrives. Only minutes after we arrived, I felt my phone vibrate in the pocket of my fireproof suit. I had it on silent but I had forgotten to turn it off. I admit that someone had informed me the year before that the use of mobile phones was strictly prohibited in the pit lane but without thinking, I dug into my pocket to turn it off. I was holding it at waist height and trying to sort it out – anyone who knows me knows that I am rubbish with phones – when an official shouted, 'Give me the phone!' I did try to explain that I wasn't trying to use it but, knowing the new rules and that phones were not allowed, I had no option but to hand it over. Of course, mobile phones are taboo under the new regulations – they might generate a spark that could cause an explosion – and I should have known better but is worth pointing out that the guy who dealt with the situation was a jobsworth of the highest order.

Shortly after the pit-lane sheriff had confiscated my phone there was announcement over the PA system that Maria Costello was being given a ten-second penalty for her pit-crew chief's use of a mobile phone. I was raging. It must have been crystal clear that I wasn't using the mobile – I had it at waist height the whole time – but he didn't think that a word in my ear was enough. I was particularly upset because the reason he'd seen the phone was that I had been trying to do the right thing by switching it off. So, after all my lecturing to the lads about being cool but slick, it ended up that I was responsible for costing Maria ten seconds before she'd even made the pit stop.

After all that, we ended up having an absolutely brilliant pit stop, one of the best of my thirty years at the TT and, of course, we didn't tell Maria about the ten-second penalty when she pitted. Time enough for the shit to hit the fan in the post-race debrief. Maria had already endured a pretty mediocre practice week before the race – she had a tired bike that repeatedly broke down on her, which had led to a pretty strained relationship between her and her mechanic. It came as no great surprise when news came though that she had actually broken down with a mechanical fault on lap three, the lap immediately after the pit stop. I was gutted for Maria but also, I have to admit, relieved that my mistake hadn't impacted on her result. I had been really hoping to help get her a personal best and a top finish because she's a bloody good pilot and a great person.

So although I welcome some of the new health and safety measures – we must always leave no stone unturned in our efforts to make road racing as safe for everyone as we possibly can – I still get concerned about the methods of implementation and about some of the personnel tasked with enforcing the rules and the way in which they carry out their duties. Some people, when they get a blazer and tie on them, get a bit full of their own importance, and no one likes a jobsworth.

Stand-out races and favourite courses

I love all the courses and they all have their individual challenges but, like everyone, I have my favourites. I love the Nationals because they are comprised mainly of local riders and there's much more of that grounded, old-school feeling about them. I will always have a soft spot for the Cookstown 100, the Tandragee 100 and the Dundrod 150 because their organisers were the first to agree to allow

Robert to make a competitive return to racing after the horrendous and career-threatening injuries he sustained in his 1994 crash. The accident left Robert quite badly disabled, with the result that he had to have the wee 125cc Honda extensively modified to enable him to race. Quite a few courses refused Robert permission to race on his modified bike, but the three I've mentioned gave him the green light. I remember that those clubs got quite a lot of stick from other quarters and people in authority but they were guided by their instinct and stuck by their decisions and Robert competed at them safely and successfully.

I have very fond memories of all three international race meetings: the North West 200, Ulster Grand Prix and Isle of Man TT. Of course, the North West 200 holds special memories for me – Robert was at his brilliant best there. He was an absolute genius on a motorbike around the triangle circuit. But those memories are tinged with sadness since it's also the circuit where he lost his life. I always try to focus on the many good times we had there, though, and his record-breaking number of victories at the race. In fact, had his bike not seized in his 2008 crash, which was not his fault, I firmly believe he would have gone on to set a record number of victories around the North West 200 circuit that no one would have bettered.

Robert had that unique Dunlop ability to jump off a 125cc machine and on to a full-blown superbike, and then jump off that and on to a 250cc bike, and win on them all – and that was back when all the races were on the same day and each class was packed with great riders. He was an incredible talent, 5'5" of road-racing genius. I'm not a big drinker but 90 per cent of the hangovers I've had in my life are associated with the North West 200. We always celebrated the victories and Robert was far better than me at that as well. He really was in a class of his own on all fronts. My only gripe about the North West is that, in my opinion, Robert was never properly rewarded financially for his world-class talent, and I don't mean in prize money. No, it was in starting/appearance money that I always felt he was short changed. Riders talk a lot to each other, and Robert knew that some of the much less talented riders from overseas were getting more starting money and expenses than Robert. That information rubbed me up the wrong way. I got the feeling that just because Robert lived just up the road in Ballymoney, and because everyone knew how much he loved the circuit, that they always presumed that he'd turn up, and they were right. But I still take exception to the fact that he didn't get the financial reward he should have. Robert was, and still is, the greatest rider I have ever seen around the North West 200 circuit.

The coast road section of the North West 200, from the Metropole to the start/finish area, is an extremely technical part of the course, where many races are won and lost. Robert was exceptional along this stretch but I have to say that, in recent years, Alastair Seeley is now the man to beat on that particular part. No surprise, perhaps, that he currently holds the record for the most wins around the triangle circuit. Glenn Irwin is another one to watch here – he has already mastered the coast road section to perfection, further highlighting the benefit of his being a top short-circuit road racer in Great Britain.

An extremely fast motorcycle can sometimes mask a rider's lack of technical ability, particularly at the North

West, where on the long straights a lesser rider can disappear into the horizon as a result of a much quicker machine. The Ulster Grand Prix is seen by many competitors as much more of a riders' circuit because bike speed is not so crucial. What is crucial is technical ability, then a fast bike. It is soul-destroying, however, particularly at the NW 200, to catch up with your main opponent on the more difficult technical sections, only to see them twist the throttle and leave you behind on the high-speed long straights.

The Ulster Grand Prix is arguably the circuit most favoured by top road racers. With no chicanes and still considered to be a pure motorcycle road race, it presents the riders with everything they work for in a transitioning road race – fast straights, fast corners and just one hairpin. Circuits like the North West 200 have changed considerably over the years but the same is not true of the Ulster Grand Prix. The Dundrod Club deserves tremendous credit for always bringing in measures – such as additional safety bales, seminars for newcomers and better medical assistance access – that improve riders' safety, and for better paddock and spectator facilities. I've seen so many fantastic races at the Ulster Grand Prix. The best 125cc race I have ever seen was there, though sadly the three riders involved are no longer with us. It was in 1993.

The race was an all-time classic – the mother of all battles between Robert, Joey and Mick Lofthouse, three absolute class acts. The lead changed several times as the three gladiators slipstreamed each other with great effect. I honestly didn't know who would win and it was one of the very few occasions that I didn't really care because, although I was a Robert man through and through, I knew

I was witnessing one of, if not the, greatest 125 road race ever. In the end, it was my man who took the chequered flag, although you could have covered all three of them with a bath towel at the finish line.

Another great race that stands out for me was one involving Joey and Robert again, Robert on the Norton and Joey on the Honda, at the Ulster Grand Prix in 1990. Speculation was rife that both would have to pit stop as neither would have enough fuel to complete the race. As expected, it was the two Dunlops who set the pace at the front, both playing their cards close to their chests with regard to their respective bike's fuel economy. It was the wily Joey who outwitted them all. When Robert pulled into the pits to refuel, Joey continued, with enough fuel left to complete and win the race.

However, Robert held a little resentment towards the UGP in later years as its organisers tried to block his racing comeback after the 1994 crash, even though the clerk of the course for the Dundrod 150 gave him the okay to compete and the UGP uses the exact same circuit. There were a couple of UGP officials that Robert didn't like – they had their views and reasons and so did Robert. I was on his side back then and, funnily enough, I still am today.

The Isle of Man TT is without doubt the toughest true test of man and machine anywhere in the world, and the race that always gave me most concern regarding Robert's safety. As soon as the TT races came around I would see a twinkle in Robert's eye, a real buzz of excitement in him and an extra spring in his step. Although I knew the thrill of racing in the TT just outweighed the fears of the circuit, it didn't stop me worrying about him from the moment we left Ballymoney until I got him back to the town in one piece. The levels of concentration required to race at the TT are enormous and only a few can focus for the entirety of a six-lap race on a superbike. Robert struggled on that front – his mind used to wander, particularly on the mountain section.

I still go to the TT every year and have enjoyed watching the likes of John McGuinness in many races there, although Michael Dunlop, Peter Hickman and Dean Harrison appear to be the new kids on the block. Currently, Hickman is the man to beat with an absolute lap record of 135.45mph.

My road racing stars

I admire every competitor who races a motorcycle – they are all heroes in my eyes – and I've been lucky enough to watch many talented riders race over the years, but everyone has their favourites. I have always been a Dunlop man but in the early days the man who really caught my eye was Raymond McCullough. He was a class act and one of our own and he is the consummate gentleman to this day. On his day he could beat Joey and several times he did. He could hold his own against the best of them, and he often did just that.

Along with Brian Reid, Trevor Steele and Ian McGregor, Raymond was a member of the Dromara Destroyers. These riders all hailed from County Down and there was a strong, competitive but friendly rivalry between them and County Antrim's Armoy Armada. The Armada included Frank Kennedy and Mervyn Robinson, as well as Jim Dunlop, but Joey was widely regarded as the flag bearer.

Raymond was very similar to Joey – quiet and unassuming and born with an immense talent for racing a motorcycle. He was the closest rival to Joey in that era.

I also had a lot of regard for another Dromara Destroyer – Brian (Speedy) Reid. Reidy was as talented a 250cc road racer as you could ever have the good fortune to see race, particularly in the mid-eighties and early nineties. He was a Formula 2 World Champion back in the day and I always rated him a class act on a 600cc machine as well – always neat and helluva fast on any road race circuit. At every race Robert and I went to, I always had Brian Reid marked down as someone we'd have to beat if we wanted to win.

Talking of world-class riders, it would be very remiss of me not to mention the one and only Phillip McCallen. Phillip will go down in history as one of the greatest ever road racers to hail from Northern Ireland, and is a multi-time winner at all the major International road races. Robert and I always considered Phillip a worthy adversary and an opponent who deserved the utmost respect. Back then all I cared about was making sure that Robert took the victory. But now that the dust has settled and I'm no longer in the thick of it it's good to be able to give Phillip the proper credit. He was world class and shone at a time when road racing was absolutely packed with bright stars. He deserves to be rated with the very best.

There is one other rider who I always rated as an extra-special road racer and that was Steve Hislop. The Flying Scotsman took on the world's best and won. He was particularly brilliant around the Isle of Man TT mountain circuit: many actually considered him to be the main threat to Joey for the 'King of the Mountain' crown. Hizzy was also a class act at all the other majors. Sadly, he lost his life in a helicopter accident but he has left a lasting legacy and an indelible mark on all true road race fans. A real star of road racing in my eyes.

It would also be impossible not to include John McGuinness, the Morecambe Missile, in my collection of greatest-ever riders. He is pure class and his world-class record backs that up. I remember one year at the Isle of Man TT having to go in the Norton recovery van to collect Robert, who had broken down near Kirk Michael. I was standing at the fast right-hander on the approach to the village during the superbike race when John came through, and he was the quickest I have ever seen through that particular section. It was then that I realised I was witnessing greatness.

Sadly a serious accident at the North West 200 in 2017 has curtailed John's chances of adding more victories at the majors. Although he's continuing to race, I don't know if he will ever get back to where he was prior to that big 'off' at Primrose Corner along the Coast Road. But one thing I can be sure of is that any time the subject of the world's greatest road racers comes up for discussion the name John McGuiness will be mentioned, and rightly so.

Currently there are two real stars from Northern Ireland who are flying the flag when it comes to short-circuit racing. They are Glenn Irwin on the British Superbike scene and Jonathan Rea in the World Superbike series. Young Glenn is a real talent and I really feel that if he can steer clear of serious injury and is provided with fast, reliable machinery, he can go on to become British Superbike champion and from there progress to the World Superbike scene. But our current biggest star from Northern Ireland is five-time World Superbike champion, Jonathan Rea. A global world superstar in the motorcycle world, he is the current jewel in the crown of Northern Ireland motorsport. He has scaled every height and overcome every hurdle and obstacle that has been put in front of him. This lad may well go down in history as Northern Ireland's greatest ever motorcycle racer and who could argue with that? Yes, of course, pure road racing supporters will always give that title to Joey Dunlop but, although short-circuit racing is a different type of discipline, there is a very sizeable number of fans who love motorcycle racing who see Jonathan Rea as our greatest ever. Johnny is a lovely lad and a great ambassador for the sport. He is a credit to his family, a credit to the sport and a credit to Northern Ireland.

But not all of my road racing stars are racers. Of all the team managers I've met my favourite is Barry Symmons. Both Joey and Robert could be complex in their own ways. For example, they tended – understandably – to withdraw and go into what I would call silent mode before a race. If you were working with them, that was a bit of a challenge. You had to become something of a mind-reader, and Barry was a master at that. Barry was at Honda with Joey and then at Norton as team boss with Robert, and he stood by both boys through thick and thin. He was a proper team boss who only ever had one face and he called a spade a spade. Symmo always had the riders' best interests at heart. He stood head and shoulders above any other team bosses. Several of the bosses of the bigger teams were very full of their own importance. They were aloof and thought they were better than many of those in the road racing family. However, Barry Symmons was as solid as you'll get, a proper star.

I'd also like to pay tribute to long-time Kawasaki team boss Jack Valentine who was and still is one of the most decent blokes you could meet in our sport – very knowledgeable and a proper gentleman, old school and down to earth.

There are stars in all areas of the sport and I want to pay particular tribute to the medics. I first met Dr Fred MacSorley at a race in the mid-eighties and from that day until this, he is a man that I hold in the very highest esteem. The Flying Doctor in his instantly recognisable orange helmet was a rock for all of us involved in motorcycle road racing. When I saw Fred at a road race I felt hugely reassured because I knew that in the event of a crash, God forbid, Fred would be on hand. I took a lot of comfort from that, and I know that riders and their families did too. Fred stabilised and saved countless numbers of injured riders. He was like a guardian angel and had the unique ability to reassure and calm people in the most difficult and critical situations.

I think the fact that Fred was a keen motorcyclist and a fan of road racing also helped. He was very much one of the road racing family and so highly respected. When Fred retired from being a 'travelling doctor' at road racing events in 2017, I was honoured to be asked to host his retirement dinner. It was a black-tie event but still very informal – bike people don't do posh gigs – held in the City Hotel in Armagh, which was full to capacity. Fittingly, the dinner was also a fundraiser for the Motorcycle Union of Ireland medical team. One of the most special parts of the evening was when I presented Fred with a card, signed by Joey and

Robert's mum, May; brother, Jim; and sisters Helen, Linda, Virginia and Margaret. It was the one and only time I saw a tear in his eye that evening. I would love to see Fred and his medical team honoured by the government for their services to the sport.

The other outstanding figure in our sport and someone who will always be a star in my eyes was also one of our travelling medics – the late great Dr John Hinds. They say appearances can be misleading and I suppose that was true of John. With his long sandy hair in a ponytail, his leathers and his deep love of road racing, he just looked like an ordinary, happy-go-lucky motorcycle enthusiast. And that is what he was, one of us, but he was also one of the top medical practitioners in Northern Ireland. Fred MacSorley was his mentor when he joined the MCUI medical team in 2003, and he told me that John was destined for the very top in the medical profession, as a superbly gifted and talented anaesthetist and intensive care consultant. Sadly, John lost his life in a fatal crash while he was carrying out his duties at the Skerries road race in County Dublin in 2015. However, he has left a lasting legacy in the Air Ambulance NI. It was John who campaigned and pushed to get this vital service up and running, and although he didn't get to see his dream become a reality, it was his drive and perseverance that made it happen. His death really brought the issue to public attention and, within the road racing family, there was a strong sense that if we could get this service established it would be a lasting tribute to John and all that he had given to the sport. It was an absolute honour for me to be asked to join William Dunlop and others to hand over a petition, signed by thousands, supporting the introduction of a Northern Ireland air ambulance service at Stormont Government Buildings in Belfast. It shouldn't go unsaid that John's family and his partner Janet Acheson worked tirelessly to support the campaign. John's memory lives on in our hearts and we will never ever forget his contribution to the sport he loved.

William Dunlop

Road racing is full of good people but William Dunlop was one of the nicest young men in the paddock, a real superstar in the making. You'd have been hard pressed to meet someone more popular or likeable. William was always extremely well-mannered, quiet and reserved, a happy-go-lucky fella who shied away from the limelight. Despite his fame, he was humble and modest – two characteristics that endeared him to many people. He was most comfortable among family and friends.

I was with Robert when William was born in 1985. We went to celebrate the birth of his first-born in a pub in Dervock, a village just outside Ballymoney. That's how, when he was only a day old, William became responsible for one of the worst hangovers I've ever had in my life. He was a beautiful child who would go on to continue the Dunlop tradition and become one of this country's greatest-ever road racers. He was talented at several sports but, given his genes, it was perhaps inevitable that his heart would lie in road racing. He loved the sport and although he was blessed with the Dunlop name, it was his unique ability, technique and talent on a motorcycle that took him to the top of his profession.

William was also an accomplished footballer, the best of the Dunlops at that sport. He was a top junior footballer and sometimes would play two games on a Saturday if he wasn't racing, and he was also a big Tottenham Hotspur fan. In 2011 I was asked to manage a legends/celebs football team in a testimonial game for former Coleraine goalkeeping legend Victor Hunter at Coleraine Showgrounds. Lots of celebrities and former footballing stars were there and I'd asked William to play in my team – he didn't look one bit out of place. Several former international footballers had turned out but the one that William really wanted to meet was former Tottenham, Manchester United and England striker, Teddy Sheringham. William, being pretty shy, didn't really want to ask Sheringham for his autograph but after the game he slipped me the Tottenham replica shirt that his mum and dad had bought for him when he was a kid and asked me if I'd get Teddy to sign it. William wouldn't push himself forward – that was just how the lad was. Teddy signed the shirt at the dinner later that night – I think he was as much in awe of William as William was of him.

William was also an excellent pool player but it was on the golf course that he and I got to spend some quality time together. He loved that sport and so do I. Every time I got the chance to play an ordinary four-ball or had the opportunity to take part in an invitation event, I rang William. All he needed to know was a time and place and he'd be there.

Because William wasn't a member of a particular club it was always difficult to nominate him a handicap number. The more he won, the more we cut his handicap, but that didn't affect his success rate. He kept winning and the others in our regular four-ball used to give him loads of stick but he always laughed his head off when he got his winnings – the princely sum of £5! William and I were always a pair in the four-ball and, fortunately, we were almost always the victors, though that was mostly down to William's talent rather than mine. William could drive the ball a mile off the tee box. Completely unorthodox in style and uncoached, he was a natural, with a wonderful eye and aptitude for ball sports.

Over the years we played many courses together. Shortly before William's death, we were playing against close friends Adrian Logan and Keith Gillespie at Galgorm Castle Golf Club on the outskirts of Ballymena, when William whispered to me, 'We're unbeaten around here for the past four years, LB.' True to form, we chinned Logie and Keith that day, and proudly claimed another fiver each in winnings.

As was the case with anyone who came into contact with him, all the staff at Galgorm became very fond of William. They asked him to become a tournament ambassador for the prestigious Northern Ireland Open Golf Tournament that was held there. William was delighted to do it. He felt very comfortable and at home at Galgorm. He much preferred the more laid-back atmosphere there to that at some of the more stuffy and pompous clubs.

He also loved Belvoir Park Golf Club in Belfast. I took him there as my guest to the Ulster Press Golf Association outing one year and he absolutely fell in love with the place. The course at Roe Park Golf Club just outside Limavady in County Londonderry also holds happy memories of William for me. There was a promo event there and we were among the guests, along with Adrian and Keith. Golf clubs have quite a strict dress code and William didn't always conform. We were VIP guests and I arrived at the club before William. I was busy explaining to the organisers that William might not arrive in fully acceptable golf attire when I noticed him breeze past in a red T-shirt with no collar and a fairly large oil stain on the front, a pair of Adidas shorts with three stripes down each side, and a pair of old trainers. It was quite clear that William had just left the garage at home where he'd been working on the bikes. I was in fits of laughter. Thankfully the golf club people were very understanding and quite prepared to turn a blind eye. William played superbly that day and I had a stinker but we still won again, thanks to him. Even my friends on the Ulster Press Golf Association who only met William a handful of times when I brought him to some of our monthly outings felt very warmly towards him. So many people were touched by his sincerity, honesty and warmth; he was just a genuine down-to-earth lad who never tried to hog the limelight.

In recent years William had become very settled and content. Ever since he had met his partner, Janine, he had showed all the signs of a young man ready to settle down and plan for his future – set up a new home and start a family – the things most young people do when they've found their perfect partner. In 2016 William and Janine's dreams came true when their baby girl Ella arrived. Two prouder parents you couldn't have found. Then, in 2018, Janine confirmed that she was pregnant again – baby number two was on its way. William and Janine were over the moon. On the home and family front, I don't think I'd ever seen William in a happier frame of mind, but on the racing scene things hadn't been going terribly well. The first major of 2018 was the North West 200 and William took a tumble at Church Corner in practice, sustaining a fairly severe back injury that led to him having to pull out of the entire meeting.

William had joined the Tim Martin (Mar-Train) Temple Golf Club race team that season and was really keen to impress. In fact, I felt that maybe he was putting himself under extra pressure. He'd ridden for several sponsors over recent years and I knew he was keen to find the perfect formula of some really fast bikes and a good team to work for. William just needed that wee change of luck; he needed reliable and fast racing motorcycles and some continuity in personnel for a sustained period of time. His ability was never in question but he'd been a victim of unreliable machinery, which had inevitably led to him changing teams too often, preventing him from building up the necessary trust within a team and with it the confidence required to win races, particularly at international level. There is no doubt whatsoever that William's poor run of luck and form over the past couple of seasons had dented his confidence.

The fact that he'd had a lean couple of years was on his mind, as was the fact that he had a young family, a family that meant the world to him. I am of the firm belief that had he seen out the 2018 season, he might well have pulled the plug on his racing career. He had spoken to me at length about this – it was clear that if he could have found an alternative way of earning a living, then he would have chosen that and spent more time with Janine and the family. I still have a text message from William from a few weeks before his death – he wanted to come and see me for a chat. I was in Belfast but told him I would be at home all of the following day if he wanted to call and he replied with the words 'Cheers LB'. That was the last contact I had with him. The next time I saw William was when the undertaker brought him home to his mum Louise's house.

The first I knew of William being involved in an accident was on the Saturday, 7 July. I was at home when I got a phone call from Barry Symmons, the former Honda and Norton chief. He told me that there had been an incident at the Skerries 100 races – he didn't know how serious but he knew it involved William. He promised to ring when he got any more information. As soon as I set my phone down, it rang again and it was my good friend Darren Crawford, a photographer with the *Ballymena Guardian* and an avid road racing fan. He asked me, 'Are you at the Skerries, LB? Is William okay?' I said I'd heard there had been an incident involving William but I didn't know any more than that. Then the phone rang again and it was my BBC sports colleague Stephen Watson to tell me that William had been involved in a bad accident – I knew that whatever had happened was very serious. And then my phone was ringing constantly. Finally, Barry Symmons called me back and suggested that it might not be such a bad idea for me to make my way to William's mother Louise's house. I asked, 'Is it bad?' and Barry said, 'Michael has just left the circuit – it's not good.'

I don't mind admitting I broke down and then immediately drove to Louise's. I could hardly see the road for tears and yet I felt numb with disbelief. As I pulled up at Louise's members of the Dunlop family circle were arriving. I didn't know what to say to this family that has suffered so much. Words seemed irrelevant. When I got in, it was a house of devastation and grief. The cause of the accident or any of the detail was not discussed. As I sat in Louise's living room, staring up at a picture of Robert, William, Michael and Daniel, the reality struck home – four were now two. Not only had we lost Joey and Robert to the sport, we had now also lost William from the next generation. My thoughts kept switching from Louise to Janine and to May, and to Michael and Daniel – I couldn't imagine how they must be feeling. For now, Janine was in the house she shared with William in Ballymoney but it was decided that the official wake was going to be in Louise's house on the Gracehill Road, a few miles outside Ballymoney, which was much bigger and better suited to coping with the crowds who wanted to come and pay their respects.

Michael had arrived home on the day that William died – he just wanted to be with his mum, his Nana May and Janine. His brother Daniel had also flown home from GB. For the next few days, I went regularly to Louise's – she had made the house open to the general public. I thought that was a brave and generous gesture and spoke volumes about her. Hundreds and hundreds of people – friends, family and fans – came to pay their respects. Friends and neighbours rallied to support the family. People were so thoughtful and kind – many brought food, and the kitchen was full of helpers all trying to make sure that everyone who called got a cup of tea, a word of thanks and something to eat.

One of the downstairs rooms was readied for William. After the accident, he had been taken to an undertaker in the south of Ireland. Although William died on the Saturday it was late the following Monday afternoon before his body was brought home. Michael had gone to meet the hearse and accompany it to Ballymoney. When the coffin arrived, the cold hard reality of William's death really hit. I still can't take it in. After the family had been in to see him, I went in. He still had that trademark slight smile on his face and I kissed his forehead and said my goodbye.

Outside in the yard, there was an eerie silence. There was a sense of disbelief, of shock among the road racing family, a sense that a line had been crossed. Some people admitted that William's death was just too much for them, that this was the end of the line for them with the sport. I know that grief often leads to knee-jerk reactions but I was struck by the number of people who came over to me and said, 'LB, that'll do me.' Some had been devoted to the sport for over forty years and were vastly experienced members of the road racing fraternity. I understood how they felt. William was such a lovely lad and it seemed so unfair that the Dunlop family would have to suffer this pain again. It was hard to make sense of anything. As we'd waited for William's body to come home, I'd had a lot of time to think and I thought it might be the end of the line for me too. I thought I probably needed to take a break, at least for a while. As I looked into the coffin it was impossible to imagine that I would never be in William's company again. I would never again see his smile, would never again have him as my trusty teammate on the golf course.

I'm sure that at least part of the reason William's death has hit me so hard is that, in many ways, he reminds me of my own son William. The two boys had a lot in common and were friends. Not only did they share a name, they were the same age and went to the same school. They grew up together, played football together. William's death reminded me in the most painful way that we take life for granted and that the things we hold dear can be taken from us in a heartbeat – it made me want to hold my own children closer, to give them an extra hug.

The funeral was on the Tuesday morning. It was decided that there would be three lifts at the funeral and I was honoured to be asked to be one of the pallbearers. Although the coffin wasn't leaving Louise's house until midday I got there early, at around 10. When I arrived with my son William, most of the Dunlop family were already there. We all wanted to spend as much time as possible with William before he set off on his final journey. It was a dull, damp day and that just about summed up the sombre mood of everyone. We all felt pretty numb as we struggled to come to terms with the realisation that this was the day of William's funeral and we would be saying goodbye to him for the final time.

At about 11.30 a.m. I went to see William for the last time and said my piece and then left to let the family have their last moments with him. I stepped outside, and stood on the front lawn. The undertakers had arrived, the hearse was in place and it was time for William to be taken to his final resting place at Garryduff graveyard, which adjoins Garryduff church just outside Ballymoney.

The journey to the church took us through the village of Dunaghy and people lined the road to pay their respects to William. It was the same in Ballymoney, with people all along the Kilraughts Road and up the Garryduff Road.

There were huge crowds outside the church and inside it was packed to the rafters. The service was simple and straightforward, as was the graveside service, and William was laid to rest with his dad and close to his Uncle Joey.

As is customary, there was a cup of tea and a bite to eat in the large adjoining church hall and hundreds of people came to pay their respects. May God bless them all for taking the time to do that – I know that it meant a lot to the family.

When the crowds had cleared, I began to make my preparations to go. It was hard to believe that the funeral was over and I was conscious that I was heading home to be with my family. My heart went out to the Dunlops.

Probably the only thing that kept me going was that I had a plan that I hoped might bring them some comfort, even in a very small way. A group of us – Adrian Logan, Stephen Watson, Albert Kirk, Joel Taggart, John Linehan and David Lewers – got together after the funeral and, with the blessing of William's family, we set about organising 'The William Dunlop Golf Classic', a golf charity fundraiser day with the proceeds going to William's family.

We held it at Galgorm Castle Golf Club, where William had been a regular. As well as the golf, we held a dinner and an auction in the evening. Many sports people contacted us, wanting to play – fellow bike riders, rugby stars like Stephen Ferris and Andy Ward, and from the world of horseracing we had several of A.P. McCoy's family. From football, we had NI Internationals Keith Gillespie, John O'Neill and Sammy Clingan. Northern Irish paralympian world record-holder and multi-gold medal winner Michael McKillop also wanted to play as did several GAA all-stars.

Big brother Lawrence and me, ready for a
football match in Ballymoney.

Signing the transfer forms from Crusaders to Drogheda as Crues secretary Harry McClelland (left), Crues manager Billy Johnston (top left) and John Cowan from Drogheda (top right) look on.

The party's in full swing after Crusaders win their first-ever League title in 1973. I'm in the back row, third from the left.

Tackling the Eintracht Frankfurt World Cup star Jürgen Grabowski in Coleraine's European Cup (Champions League) game in Germany in 1975.

Last-minute words of encouragement to my favourite road racer of all time, the great Robert Dunlop.

On the winners' podium at the Isle of Man TT with the two main men, Robert and Joey Dunlop.

In Gasoline Alley, ready for refuelling duties at the Isle of Man TT.

With a 22mm ring spanner, checking Robert's rear-wheel spindle
after changing the gearing.

Laying flowers and a specially laminated card from Joey's mum and family at Joey's memorial in Tallinn in Estonia in July 2015.

Gavan Caldwell

A young William Dunlop – not far from my side, as usual –
as we make our way to meet his father Robert at the North West 200.

Darren Crawford

Three really good friends who helped me organise the William Dunlop
Golf Classic – (L–R) Albert Kirk, John Linehan and Adrian Logan.

Many celebrities and sports personalities, including Rory McIlory, Michael O'Neill and Jonathan Rea, contacted us to offer either sports experiences or signed merchandise to be auctioned either on the night or on social media.

On the night of the dinner the function room at Galgorm Castle was packed. We were honoured that almost thirty of the Dunlop family attended the evening, including Louise, Janine, and William's nana, May. Louise and Janine joined me on stage at the end of the night to say thank you to everyone who had contributed in any way to making the day such a success. In the end, we raised three times the amount we had hoped for from the golf and the auction.

Pouring all of my energies into the fundraising did make me feel as if I could at least do something to help. It made me feel less powerless and helpless but I was still struggling to come to terms with William's death and with my own relationship to road racing. I still find it difficult to accept the fact that William's gone, that he's not going to be out on the golf course with me, that he won't be taking my gripper bag to the Isle of Man, as he did every year. Small things remind me constantly that he's gone. The loss of Robert and Joey shook me, shook the entire road racing community and this country to its foundations, but they were both forty-nine when they passed. They were taken too soon but they'd had a reasonable life. William was only starting out, he had another baby on the way, a new house – he was just so happy. When the sport that I loved so much took him away, it broke something in me, and I had to walk away for a while.

The decision was accelerated by the fact that I had been contracted to commentate on the Ulster Grand Prix in

August 2018, just a month after William's death. I had to ask myself whether I could go into a commentary box and give of my best and sound excited when I was still heartbroken? The BBC in no way pressurised me into making a decision, and fully understood my feelings at that time – I felt duty-bound to be honest and admit that I couldn't bring myself to do the commentary or the sport any justice, given how I was feeling.

The road race season was almost over, which was another factor. I thought, if I take a break now, I'll only miss one major race. I was thinking about the people in the sport and was conscious that they deserved better than I was able to give them at that moment. I was also aware that I needed to look after myself. The commentary box at the Ulster Grand Prix overlooks the start/finish line and the grid – looking down and seeing a space where William would have been would have had me in tears. I could well have had to leave the commentary box and that would have been totally unprofessional.

Because of my commentary duties with the BBC, my decision to take a break from the sport ended up becoming public. I knew it would be and I didn't really mind that. I've never had a problem giving my honest opinion about anything or telling people how I feel. I was broken-hearted and I needed a break, and I was okay with saying that to people. One rider, Ryan Farquhar, criticised me for going public. I know of the man but I don't know him personally and, given his comments, all I will say is that he most definitely does not know me.

For a long time, I didn't know if I'd ever go back to road racing. I couldn't imagine sitting in the BBC commentary box sounding excited about any race. It was a very strange feeling – I still loved the sport and the road racing family but I was angry about William's death and I didn't know who to blame. The Dunlop family were – and still are – a tower of strength to me. It should have been me comforting them but often it was the other way around. They understood that I needed time and they respected that.

It took the best part of nine months for me to decide to go back into road racing. After some heartfelt conversations with William's mum, Louise, and with other members of the Dunlop family, plus long talks with my own family and close friends and others involved in the sport, I decided in early March that I felt able to attend and commentate at road races again. I hadn't attended a race since William passed but I never stopped loving the sport and being part of it. One of the things that really convinced me to go back was the argument that you can only improve something if you are part of it. And I knew there were areas in the sport to which I could perhaps help to bring improvements. I also know that road racing is my home, my family.

One of the positive things that came of stepping away was that it gave me a bit of perspective, a chance to try and see the big picture. That time brought me face to face with a few home truths. When I thought about it, I realised that when there was an incident, I, like a good many people, had a tendency to shake my head and, while I felt sympathy and sorrow for those involved and all who were close to them, I was quick to think that that was just the way it was, that there was nothing that could be done about it. It was easier to move on, to pretend that it wouldn't happen again.

But in 2018, it became increasingly difficult to do that. It was a dreadful year for the sport. We lost six riders – James Cowton, Alan 'Budd' Jackson, Fabrice Miguet, Dan Kneen, Adam Lyons and William Dunlop. I can't remember a year like it for fatalities. And that's not including the riders who suffered serious injuries. It felt like the sport was at a crossroads or that I was at a crossroads with the sport.

In the last year I've done a lot of soul-searching and I'm glad to be back and taking an active role once again. But my focus has changed and I'm no longer willing to accept that 'that's just the way things are' when it comes to the safety of riders. I'm committed to trying to make the sport safer in whatever way possible, particularly for up-and-coming riders. I'm currently involved in discussions to get one of the smaller race meetings back up and running, part of a wider strategy to provide more racing opportunities on short circuits for young riders.

I was encouraged by a report in June 2019 from the Northern Ireland Motorsport Taskforce. Set up by the Stormont Executive in 2017, the taskforce was established to look at the contribution of motorsports to the culture and economy of Northern Ireland, and to develop an action plan to maximise the potential of motorsports here. I was consulted by the chair of the taskforce, Ian Paisley, and gave my feedback before its official publication in June 2019. Road racing was only one strand within the report, but the overall focus on safety, on paths of progression for young people within motorsports and on a more strategic and collaborative approach was impressive and made a lot of sense to me. It's early days yet but we now need actions to go with these words.

Of course, the governing bodies and custodians of road

racing have a significant role to play in assisting with the implementation of the taskforce report. Perhaps road racing needs its own separate, independent taskforce to look more strategically at ways of improving safety and at other crucial aspects of the sport. The road racing family cannot continue to stumble from one year to another, shaking our heads and doing nothing. We still have too many amateurs controlling affairs within the sport. And this is much too dangerous a sport for us to be able to afford an amateurish approach to the future.

PART TWO BALLS

Kicking a ball about

From a very young age, in fact as far back as I can remember, I loved kicking a ball about. I spent almost all my time playing football, whether out in the street or in one of the fields nearby. No matter what shape or condition it was in, a ball could keep up to thirty of us kids amused for hours on end. With a couple of coats or jumpers thrown down for goalposts, it was game on.

It was when I went to the local primary school, the Model in Ballymoney, and began playing football there that I realised I wasn't too bad at it. A teacher took me to one side and told me to keep at the football as he felt I could make a living at it. He was a kind man and he made me feel special that day. I played right through primary school and for much of secondary school, for all the various age groups.

But, although I played a lot of football at home and at school, I always had to borrow a pair of boots to play in. I never had a pair of my own – we couldn't afford them. My family was very working class, and proud of it, but there wasn't much money about. I lost my father, Jim, when I was two – he died of a brain haemorrhage when he was only twenty-six – and times were especially tough after that. Money was tight and luxuries were non-existent. At Christmas my mum, Maud, always did her best to get me and my big brother, Lawrence, one main toy – for me it was usually a new football – and a knee-length school sock that contained three or four pieces of fruit. That was it.

I never really enjoyed school and I mitched off as much as I could: in one term alone I had forty absences. I had a chip on my shoulder and a short temper and got into fights at school at least once a week. The world was against me, or so I thought. In retrospect, I can see that I was full of pent-up anger and frustration at having lost my father and I was worried about my mum and how she was going to make ends meet. I resented those who were better off and who didn't have to worry about money in the way we did.

But then, in 1965, when I turned fourteen – school-leaving age back then was fifteen – I got picked to play for the Northern Ireland football team. It was a great honour, although I still didn't own a pair of boots. My family said I couldn't play for my country in borrowed boots, so my mum and five uncles and aunts all chipped in ten bob (50p) each and took me to Bishops shoe shop in Coleraine to buy me a brand-new pair of black-and-white Adidas boots. They cost £2.50. There was ten bob over, which they told me I could keep as pocket money, since my very first game as part of the Northern Ireland set-up was an away match in Manchester. I was in a state of shock because I'd never had so much to spend at one time in my whole life. I was pleased as punch as I headed off on the boat with the rest of the team.

I was a like a fish out of water. The other young lads weren't unfriendly but I didn't find it that easy to mix with them. I was always conscious of my broad north Antrim accent, particularly as the team was mostly made up of city players – they probably wouldn't have understood a word I said anyhow. Also, I hadn't really travelled at all and the trip to Manchester was my first time out of Northern Ireland. The whole experience was pretty new for me and I felt a bit out of my depth and ill at ease.

We stayed in a dormitory and the manager had instructed

us all to have lights out and be in bed by 9 p.m. I did as I was told but most of the others were sliding up and down the floor, 'acting the lig' and carrying on. I lay awake for some time and thought about how I'd spend my money. In the end I decided to buy my mum an ornament – they used to be all the go back then. She had taken on two jobs – working as a farm labourer during the day and then cleaning houses in the evening – just to provide for Lawrence and me, to pay the bills and put a loaf of bread on the table. But, in the morning, as I headed to the canteen with the rest of the team for breakfast, I discovered that my ten bob was gone. Some of my so-called teammates had nicked it out of my trouser pocket while I was sleeping. I was shell-shocked but I told no one. I spent the remainder of the trip penniless. Every time we went into town or down the street and the other team members went into a sweet shop, or whatever, I stood outside. I only ate when the team had their official meals. Bang went my mother's ornament. I didn't even tell her or my family when I got home – I was too embarrassed – but the whole thing left a bad taste in my mouth. I couldn't get my head around how any teammate could be so low as to steal from another.

Before I went to Manchester, I'd thought that there might be a future for me in the sport, that I might be able to make a living from football, but that trip really soured things. It knocked my love for the sport and for some of those involved in it. So, when an apprenticeship in plumbing and heating came up, I didn't feel too sad about walking away from football to accept it. A football career, I knew, could be shortlived, but in those days, having a trade was seen as the pinnacle of success – a job for life.

The apprenticeship was with Ballymoney firm Donaghy Bros but I was actually based in the Creggan housing estate in Londonderry. Every day was a long day. I had to be on site and ready to start working by 8 a.m. but, since there were no bypasses between Ballymoney and Londonderry back then and my only mode of transport was a tired old van, I had to leave Ballymoney every morning at about 6.30 a.m. Quitting time was 5 p.m., so I wasn't getting home till about 7 p.m. I'd get in and have my supper, then it was practically time for bed. That was how it was, five days per week (including Friday as we didn't finish early) and every day we worked the full quota of hours on site. I pretty much turned my back on my football career, and I don't really recall missing it. Also, I had other responsibilities. When I was seventeen, I married my long-term girlfriend June and, not too long after, we had a daughter, Louise. It was a hectic time across the board.

Crusaders FC

It wasn't until five years later, in 1971, when I had served my apprenticeship, that I got any proper time to think about football again. One night I agreed to play in a summer league game in Garvagh, County Londonderry, with a few mates from Ballymoney 'toon'. After the game, Colm McFeely, right-back for Belfast Premier League club Crusaders, asked if I'd like to go to Belfast the following week for a trial with his team. Irish League football would be time-consuming, so I told him I'd think about it, but I knew that at twenty years of age, if I was ever going to make the move into senior football it had to be then. The extra money would be handy too!

So, that next week I went up to Crusaders' ground. I wasn't too sure what to expect and, understandably, I was nervous – I was a country lad with a broad accent entering the lions' den of Irish League football at a Belfast club. I trained that next week and was asked to play for the reserves, managed by Norman Pavis, who was an absolute legend at the club. Norman was a gentleman – and what a player! – but he was a proper hard man as well and we got on like a house on fire. In the end I played only one game for Crusaders Reserves as the next week I got called aside at training and told by manager Billy 'Jonty' Johnston that I was in the first team squad for the Saturday away game to Cliftonville FC at their home ground, Solitude. I couldn't believe it – after two weeks training and one reserve team game, I was now being promoted to the first team. The speed of it all made it feel a bit unreal but it was a dream come true. I'll never forget the day I signed the contract, especially when I read that the club would pay me £7 per week – yes, a massive £7! It was more than I was getting in wages as a plumber and, boy, did I know how much difference £7 per week would make to me and my family.

I didn't sleep a wink the Friday night before my debut game, even though I was convinced I would only be on the bench as sub (back then, in Irish League football, a team was only allowed one sub, not the seven that teams are allowed nowadays). On the day of the game, however, as all of us players walked across the pitch at Solitude, Billy Johnston called me over, put his arm around me and said, 'You're starting today, son.' I almost shit a brick. This all felt more serious, more professional. It's a small thing, but I remember when it was my turn to get a leg massage from our physio and trainer, Harry McGaw, that I really felt like a proper player for the first time.

I was picked to play inside-forward – my right foot and left foot were pretty equal and so I could play either the right or left – which is fairly high up the pitch as a midfield player. The centre-forward that day was Irish League legend Sammy 'Save Us' Pavis (Norman's brother) and, as we were waiting for the game to start, he walked over to me and said, 'If you're looking to find me with the ball today, son, I'll be stood around this area,' and he pointed to the penalty spot. We won the match – Sammy Pavis scored at least one goal and, from memory, I played pretty well – and that was my professional football career up and running.

Billy Johnston was building a really good side, and I was lucky to be part of it. Crusaders were, and still are, a physical team and some of the players would have cut you in two in a tackle – they aren't called the 'Hatchet Men' for nothing – but that suited me just fine. I was the left full-back and I didn't mind in the slightest if the game cut up a bit rough – I quite relished a chance to 'mix it' any way the opposition fancied it. As my friend Harry Gregg advised me, 'Always retaliate first.' That being said, Crusaders could also play technically, if that was what was required, and the team had its share of technically-gifted players. Jackie Fullerton was one of those – he had a magic wand of a left foot and a great eye for a goal. During his time at Crusaders he scored some memorable and important goals for the club.

Jackie signed just after me, and we hit it off immediately. From the first moment he walked into the dressing room, we gelled – we had a similar sense of humour and were both from the country – and he is still my dear friend today. In fact, it was thanks to Jackie that I discovered my sheepskin coat was a fake. Back then, all the professional footballers wore sheepskin coats – they were the 'in' thing – and one day I lifted Jackie's coat off the peg in the dressing room by mistake. I nearly dropped it, it was so heavy – it must have been at least four times heavier than mine, though the man at Nutts Corner market who'd sold it to me had assured me it was the real McCoy. Conned again, Beckett!

Joining Crusaders was the best thing I ever did in football. The team was packed with good players, but there were no prima donnas or Billy Big Times, just a group of honest-to-goodness footballers who would have gone through a brick wall and more for the club. Our goalkeeper was Terry 'Nicky' Nicholson, who was a great shot-stopper; Colm McFeely was an excellent right full-back; I had now slotted in to the left full-back position. The half-back line was superb: skipper Walter McFarland was right-half; John Flannagan was centre-half; and the left-half was John McPolin, a Rolls Royce of a man – big, smooth and quiet. The brilliant Bobby McQuillan was right-wing; the quiet man, Laurie Todd, was inside-right; Tom Finney was centre-forward; Jackie Fullerton was inside-left; and Charlie Tuson was the left winger. Sometimes that line-up changed but not very often. The camaraderie in the dressing room and on the field of play was as good as it ever gets. We were a family, and nobody could do anything to a member of this family and get away with it.

At the start of the 1972/73 season I had a feeling we would do okay, but I never could have anticipated how magnificent the season would be. It's every footballer's dream to win a league title and it was mine, though I knew we'd be up against it to deliver that. Linfield and Glentoran were the Belfast 'Big Two' back then, and rightly so. Both teams were packed with quality players and strength in depth. But we started the season really well and put points on the board early. Everyone expected Linfied and Glentoran, in particular, to reel us in over the marathon of a season and they expected us to falter, but we never did. We turned Seaview into a fortress and went through the whole season unbeaten at home, which was unprecedented for the Crues.

I remember on the very last day of the season we played against Larne, a bloody tough and uncompromising team, at Inver Park. We needed to beat them to be sure of winning the league, and we did, taking the victory 5–2 on the day. Winning the league was an incredible achievement for Crusaders, one of the so-called smaller clubs, and it was the first time in the club's history that we had brought home the Gibson Cup, the most prestigious trophy in Irish League football.

The scenes of jubilation at the final whistle are something I will never forget. Grown men were crying their eyes out as the Crues fans rushed the pitch. My family were all there, and the joy and elation on my mum's face meant so much to me – we'd come through so many hard times together and I was delighted to have made her so proud. I think our celebrations went on until the following afternoon – I can't remember when my mum and the rest of the family went home, but my big brother Lawrence and my Uncle Hughie stayed on to the end. I can't remember most of it, to be honest, though I do know a lot of us went back to Billy Johnston's house where Billy produced a few beers and his wife, Iris, made us some grub. God knows what state we left the house in.

One of the most memorable games I ever played in was when we were pushing for that league title. We were up against one of the top Belfast clubs and we were just heading out of the dressing room for the second half. As I went to leave, Billy said to me, 'Liam, ask Nicky if he wants a cap.' Nicky was our goalkeeper, Terry Nicholson. There was strong sun that day, and Billy was concerned that it might blind Nicky, making high balls difficult to see. As I came out of the tunnel on to the edge of the pitch, in view of the massive crowd, I called to Nicky, who had already taken up his position in goal, 'Do you want a cap?' But the crowd was quite loud, and he was struggling to hear what I was saying. I tried to signal to him, moving my right hand in an up and down fashion at my forehead, when suddenly I heard a voice from the home stand shout, 'I told you he was a Fenian fucker.' He thought I was making the Sign of the Cross.

That comment, however, was also a reference to the fact that I am called Liam. My actual name is William but I was christened Liam – which is a name much more common in the Catholic community. I come from a family of staunch Protestants and unionists, so why my dad decided on that name I don't know, but it has taken me down many an avenue that might otherwise have been closed to me. It's also brought me some unwelcome attention from time to time. I regularly faced a tirade of sectarian abuse at certain football stadiums – for years during my career I was called a 'Fenian bastard' by many opposition supporters, who thought that I was a Catholic just because of my name. I never let it annoy me too much.

That day in Belfast I was playing at one of the tougher, predominantly Protestant, clubs and I suppose the home supporters thought that I was deliberately trying to antagonise them. In no time, all hell had let loose and they were throwing stones and all sorts of objects at me.

Eventually, calm was restored, and the match continued, though every time I got the ball there was a chorus of boos, hoots and whistles. Crusaders went on to win the game and, after the final whistle, things took a turn for the worse. We were all in the communal tub after the match – there were few showers in dressing rooms back then – when I heard strange voices in the dressing room. RUC officers were there to let us know that a few opposition supporters had formed a lynch mob outside the ground and were looking for me. Losing the game had been bad enough for them, and they were also seething because they thought I had blessed myself in front of the main grandstand. The police insisted that I could not leave the stadium in the team coach – it would jeopardise the safety of the other players – so the decision was made to smuggle me out in a black taxi with blacked-out windows.

I was bundled into the back seat, out of sight of the main gate and the assembled mob, and told to lie flat until we were clear of the stadium. The hope was that the mob would be more focussed on the team coach because that's where they thought I'd be. I'll never forget the taxi driver, a craggy-faced, hardened guy, leaning back and saying to me, 'Don't get up until I tell you. By the way my name's

Vincent,' – another Catholic name. I remember saying back to him, 'For Christ's sake, don't you start as well.' I did exactly as instructed and we were soon clear of the grounds. The RUC informed the mob that I'd already left, and the team bus left the stadium without incident.

Of course, all the drama was worth it when we took home the Gibson Cup later that season. We were on a high. We felt unstoppable, and that August, just for good measure, we also went on to win the short-lived Carlsberg Cup.

At the beginning of the following season, however, the team began to break up. Fullerton went to UTV to join the sports team there – we kept him going that he was going into the movie business; Colm McFeely left; Tom Finney and Charlie Tuson got transferred to English League clubs. Billy signed some good replacements, though – players like goalkeeper Roy McDonald; Geoff Gorman who was an excellent full-back; Geordie Lennox, a left-winger, who'd come from Distillery; and Drew Cooke, a right full-back, who arrived from Coleraine. I reckoned we'd still be okay.

However, we still had the European Cup games (now the UEFA Champions League) to contend with. Back then, there were no qualifying games like they have now. No, you went straight in with the big boys, the best that Europe had to offer.

Crusaders were drawn against the crack Romanian team, FC Dinamo Bucureşti, which was packed with world-class players, and full internationals at that. The first game was at home and we played at Windsor Park to accommodate the big crowd. We lost the game 1–0 but we'd come close to scoring – the ball had hit the crossbar – and I remember thinking Dinamo weren't all they were cracked up to be, and that we were in with a genuine chance of beating them next time. Even when we found out that we had only played their reserve team – apparently, they'd wanted to save their big guns for the home leg in Romania – I still thought we'd tell them a few home truths when we got over there. I did some radio and newspaper interviews before we left for Romania and I remember saying, 'This ain't over yet!'

When we arrived in Bucharest, we were chauffeured everywhere by luxury coach. We had all been issued with new team clothing and travelling bags so we really looked the part. We went to the Dinamo stadium, Stadion Dinamo, the day before the game and were allowed to watch Dinamo train before they came off and we went on. I noticed that this squad looked much bigger and played much better than the Romanian players who had come to Belfast, but I still tried to convince myself that we'd be fine. After all, we were league champions, we were the best team in our country, just as Dinamo were in Romania. To the best of my knowledge, they didn't even stay behind to watch us train. That should have started the alarm bells ringing, but it didn't.

We arrived at the stadium on the day of the game to a heroes' welcome from the Romanian fans. I think they were very sympathetic towards us because the Troubles at home were at their very worst then, lots of shootings and bombings. We walked the whole way around the inside of the stadium on the running track, all dressed in our team suits, and waving to the thousands of fans. The heat was stifling, but I was so caught up in the occasion that I paid little heed. It all felt a bit surreal. As we walked around the track, lapping up the applause from the Romanian fans, there was a special women's match being played on the main stadium pitch as a prelude to the big game.

Kick-off was at 7.30 p.m. and, as we lined up, I remember thinking how big and physical the members of the Dinamo squad looked. They were world-class, full-time professional footballers and, as such, they spent a lot of time in the gym on the weights. The big guy I was up against was built like a shithouse, absolutely rippling with muscles, but I was always game. 'C'mon ahead, big lad, I'll have you,' I thought.

Billy Johnston had continuously hammered the message home to us not to give the ball away cheaply: 'While we have the ball, they can't hurt us.' Good solid advice, but in the thick of the action, it's much easier said than done. We lost the ball at the bloody kick-off. Someone passed it back to me but only half-hit the pass – a 'hospital' ball as it was quite often known. As I went to meet it, I could see the Dinamo guy marking me doing likewise. He was busting a gut to get there first, but we both got there about the same time and he hit me harder than I've ever been hit in my life. I bounced to my feet right away, but I saw stars for about ten minutes.

Dinamo scored in the first ten minutes and, before we could even collect ourselves, they were four up. We then stupidly began attacking wildly, trying to score, and they mercilessly picked us off. I can remember one hilarious moment in the game (yes, there was one) when I looked up at the giant electronic scoreboard in the stadium and it read 9–0. Our left half, John McPolin, ran past me, his tongue bouncing off his kneecaps, and I casually asked him, 'Is that the score or the time?' He collapsed in a heap laughing. When we came into the dressing room after the match Billy had a go at the pair of us – he wanted to know why two of his players were in hysterics and what we had found so funny about getting a trouncing. When John told Billy and the dressing room what I'd said, everyone fell about laughing. Well, we'd just got hammered and for a few minutes it lifted our spirits.

We flew back to Belfast the following day, and as we walked through the airport we read the headlines on the newspaper advertising boards: 'Crusaders – lambs to the slaughter'. It was only when I got home and studied the Dinamo team properly that I realised it was packed with vastly experienced international football stars. It was a hugely humiliating defeat for us as Irish League champions, and it certainly highlighted the vast difference between part-time Irish League footballers and world-class, full-time professional players.

Drogheda United FC

One clear evening in 1973, when I was training at Seaview, Billy Johnston tapped me on the shoulder and gave me news that I never dreamt I would hear. 'The club have accepted an offer for you from Drogheda United in the League of Ireland, Liam. The Drogheda manager is here tonight to speak to you.'

The news hit me like a bombshell. I was so happy at Crusaders. I loved the club and the people – it was just like my second home. We were current League Champions and Carlsberg Cup holders – why would I want to leave? I'd had a great season and I'd wanted to spend the rest of my career on the Shore Road, but that option had been taken away from me. Billy explained that Drogheda had come into some money and wanted to sign five players from the Irish League in an attempt to win major silverware south of the border. It was a good chance for me to earn real good money.

I felt numb as I walked off the training pitch and headed to the Crusaders boardroom to meet the Drogheda people – manager, John Cowan, and their agent, Arthur 'Mousey' Brady, a former Crusaders and Derry City legend. Also at the meeting was Crusaders chairman, Derek Wade, a man who was always more than good to me. They explained that my wages with Drogheda would be £40 per week, a hefty increase on the £7 per week I was earning at Crusaders, plus I would get a four-figure signing-on fee. I was blown away by the deal and, coming from a family where money was scarce, I was immediately tempted. But this was the early seventies, and the Troubles were at their absolute worst. Crossing the border was not for the faint-hearted, believe me. So I asked the Drogheda party to give me twenty-four hours to consider their offer as I wanted to talk it over with my mum. June and I had parted not long before that but I still had our two children, Louise and Lawrence, to consider. I needed time to think everything through, especially since the offer had come as something of a shock.

John Cowan explained to me that they needed five new players and they'd already signed four. Danny Trainor, an outstanding Crusaders midfield player who lived in Ardoyne; Distillery's Martin Donnelly, a top midfielder from the Falls; Geordie O'Halloran, a top left-winger who lived in Beechmount; and former Glentoran striker, Gerry McCaffrey, also Belfast-based. They were all Catholics, but I failed to notice that at the time. I was the last piece of the jigsaw, they said.

I discussed the Drogheda signing with my mum at length and, although the extra money was tempting, she was extremely concerned that I would be a target for terrorists. Back then Northern Ireland was volatile and polarised. You were either Protestant or Catholic and there wasn't a lot of love lost between the two. The border was a hotspot – I would be crossing it regularly, a Protestant playing for an Irish team, Nevertheless, Crusaders had already agreed to accept Drogheda's offer, so it felt like it was time to move on. I accepted the transfer. The fact that I'd be playing in a much more professional set-up didn't concern me in the slightest but, given the magnitude of the Troubles, crossing the border did.

The games down south were always played on a Sunday, and the plan was that we would travel down on a Saturday morning, but for my first home game, the club directors asked me to come down on the Friday as they wanted to introduce me to some people. They paraded me down the big main street, like an auld heifer they'd bought at the market, introducing me to all the shopkeepers. As we neared the lower end of town, they led me in the direction of a big Catholic church, took me right to its front doors and invited me in.

'Why are you taking me in here?' I asked one of the Drogheda directors nervously. I had no problem at all going into the church but I knew if it was reported or photographed it wouldn't go down too well at home.

'Saint Oliver Plunkett's head is here, kept inside a glass case,' he said. 'We want you to see it.'

It was at that moment that the penny dropped and I realised that they thought I was a Catholic – all the other Belfast players they had signed were Catholic and I guessed they'd signed me on the assumption that I was too. As they took turns walking me round Oliver Plunkett's head, I decided the best thing to do was just to play along – to say nothing and not let on I was a Prod. Then, just as we were about to leave the church, I caught a glimpse of some photographers waiting outside. I knew that if the Northern Ireland papers printed a picture of me coming out of a Catholic church, chances were I'd be hung from the nearest tree when I returned to Ballymoney. So, I asked one of the caretakers if there was a side door and made my exit. The snappers never got their picture. But I knew at that moment that I was in deep shit. How long could I keep it a secret that I was a Protestant?

I kept quiet and played my first game on the Sunday without incident – from memory, we won 2–1 and I played okay. The following week, however, when we were all travelling down south for the game together in a minibus driven by Mousey Brady, everyone, including Mousey, started singing rebel songs. 'The Ballad of Billy Reid', 'Four Green Fields', 'Rifles of the IRA', 'Men Behind the Wire', you name it, they were singing it – and there I was, in the middle of the bus, singing away at the top of my voice along with the rest. I remember thumping the sides of the bus with my fist to conceal the fact that I didn't know the words. It was bedlam and I was doing everything I could to keep up the pretence that I was Catholic. The sweat was pouring off me and we hadn't even played the game yet.

The third week we were all in the minibus again, making our way towards Drogheda. I was freezing so I shouted to Mousey, 'Arthur, can you turn the heater on? I'm foundered.'

He couldn't hear me because of the noise, but big Danny Trainor who was sat on my left side said, 'We can't turn the heater on, Becks, the butter will melt.'

Well, I knew my north Antrim accent was broad, and Jackie Fullerton had always advised me to speak slowly and clearly, so I thought right away that Danny hadn't heard me properly. I slowed it down and said again, 'Arthur, can you turn the heater on please? I'm freezing.'

But Danny piped up again, 'It's okay, Becks, I heard you the first time. They can't put the heat on or the butter will melt.'

'What butter?' I asked.

Danny replied, 'Do you not know? Look below the seats!'

And when I looked, the space under every seat was packed with Dromona butter, which was much more expensive in the south than the north. The bastards were smuggling it across the border! I was gobsmacked.

So, three weeks into my signing for Drogheda United and there I was, a man from a staunchly Protestant family steeped in the unionist tradition, all of whom were supporters of either Glasgow Rangers or Linfield (or both) – and I'd already been to chapel, learned quite a few rebel songs back to front, and was now smuggling bloody butter. When I look back, it's hilarious, but back then it was deadly serious. We were regularly taken out of the bus at army stops, put up against the wall and searched from head to toe, and shootings and bombings were practically everyday events. I can still remember Mousey having to drive the minibus up over footpaths to get around burning buses and barricades in Belfast. It seems crazy and scary now, but back then it was normal.

It was during my fourth week at Drogheda that my cover was blown. We'd just got into our home dressing room at Lourdes Stadium, and I was hanging up my fake sheepskin coat, when that wee shite Mousey announced to the whole dressing room, 'By the way, lads, yer man in the corner is a Jaffa!' – one of the words used back then for a Protestant or an Orangeman. There was complete silence for about ten seconds and then all hell let loose with the banter and slagging. The funny thing is that, once the shit had hit the fan, I couldn't have been treated better. As the only Prod, I became something of a novelty and the craic was mighty. When we were getting frisked by the soldiers at the various random checkpoints the other players used to shout to the soldiers, 'Let him be, he's one of yous!'

Every Sunday before our home games at the Lourdes Stadium a brass band used to parade around the pitch, playing the Republic's national anthem – I always stood as a mark of respect. Even though it wasn't my anthem, I was in another country and earning a living there so I had no problem whatsoever in recognising and respecting the home anthem. For me, that's how it should be when you're in any country. One of the women in the band took a shine to one of my teammates. After every game, she arrived at the dressing room with a large home-baked apple tart. We always ate it on the way home that night, to save any questions from his wife. We always gave him dog's abuse about that apple tart!

One particular game with the team that really sticks in my mind was an away Cup game against Cork Celtic FC, a crack team of top-class players. The stadium, Turners Cross, was packed that night, and right from the first whistle we were under intense pressure. It seemed only a matter of time before Cork Celtic would score, and so they did. A cross came into our penalty area for the umpteenth time and the big Celtic centre-forward – a tough guy called Ben Hannigan – rose above everyone else and buried his header into the corner of our net.

It was clearly a goal, but incredibly the ball had gone into the corner of our net and passed through a small gap where the net hadn't been secured tightly enough to the goalpost. The ball had come to rest outside the net and, unbelievably, the referee gave us a goal kick. All hell let loose. Hannigan went ballistic and I had to restrain him from ripping the head off the poor referee, who had obviously made a horrendous mistake. The Cork Celtic players were all going crazy and so were their fans – in no time they were throwing stones and the odd golf ball. The referee went over and spoke with the Cork officials and made it clear that, if the missiles didn't stop, he would have to consider abandoning the game. No sooner had the match restarted than I felt a swish of air go past my head. I didn't know what it was until one of my teammates shouted, 'Stop the game!' Then he showed me a large dart that had just missed me. It was a big beast of a dart and could have put my eye out or caused considerable damage had it connected. It was a bloody lucky let-off and one that still brings me out in goosebumps when I think about it. Once the referee got wind of the dart attack, that was enough for him and he immediately called a halt to proceedings, which probably saved our bacon – there was no way we were going to win that match that day.

One of the most bizarre incidents of my football career also happened when I was playing for Drogheda. We were playing against Dublin team Shamrock Rovers FC in the League of Ireland. I was taking my own car to the game and my big brother, Lawrence, and two other mates – Paddy 'Mohair' Dunlop and Joe 'Jobo' McVicker – decided to come with me, to keep me company on the journey. We travelled down to Drogheda on the Saturday, the day before the game, and the lads stayed in the same hotel that the club used for the players.

I went to bed fairly early, as I always did the night before a game, while Lawrence, Paddy and Jobo went to the hotel bar. I was woken in the early hours of the morning by a rumpus outside my room. I went out to investigate and, to my horror, discovered my brother in a confrontation with another male guest. Lawrence, who had made full use of the bar, had got his room number wrong and had jumped into bed beside this other poor man who had been sound asleep but had forgotten to lock his door. Eventually the man, the hotel manager and I finally got Lawrence into his own room, along with Paddy and Jobo, who were also pretty well on. I let the three of them know my feelings the next morning at breakfast and they were extremely apologetic and remorseful, but I knew only too well that the hotel manager would report the incident to the club and I'd get a rap on the knuckles over it.

As it was match day, I made my way to meet up with the rest of the team for our usual pre-match lunch and prep/team talk. Lawrence, Paddy and Jobo planned to go for a walk through the town to take in the sights before they went to the game. With us playing Shamrock Rovers, the Lourdes Stadium was packed and rocking. It was a big game, but we were ready for battle. About halfway through the first half, the game was evenly poised at 0–0 when the referee blew the whistle. I couldn't see what was going on, so I turned to my centre-half partner and teammate Willie Roche and asked him, 'Why has the ref stopped the game?' to which he replied, 'There's some idiot on the pitch – a spectator has jumped the fence.'

Willie and I walked slowly towards the halfway line to see what was going when I suddenly thought, hang on a minute, that's my bloody brother, Lawrence. He was staggering down the middle of the pitch towards me carrying something in his hand. I was mortified.

The ref and some players were pleading with him to leave the pitch immediately and two police officers were in hot pursuit as well. Everyone was shouting, 'Get off the pitch, you idiot!' and Lawrence was shouting back, 'Get to fuck, I'm only here to give something to my brother, Liam.'

Eventually we met near the centre circle and I said, 'Lawrence, what the flip are you doing?' – or words to that effect. Lawrence handed me a burger. 'Here,' he said, 'I thought you might need that – you must be famished.' It turned out the three lads had decided against a morning of sightseeing and had gone to the bar instead. All three were completely plastered. Lawrence had decided that, because they all felt hungry, maybe I did too. I suppose he was only doing what he'd been doing all his life, looking after his kid brother, but oh my God I was so embarrassed.

They finally got Lawrence off the pitch and out of the ground – apparently he was singing a Roy Orbison classic the entire time – and the match was restarted. It actually ended scoreless, but the talk afterwards was of the game being stopped because a spectator had decided to make his way on to the pitch to present one of the players with a burger. The rest of the players gave me a real ribbing for a long time afterwards, but the club were not amused. They summoned me to a board meeting the following week and let me know in no uncertain terms that this type of behaviour was totally unacceptable, and that one more incident of a similar nature would lead to my sacking.

Of course, I still love my big bro to bits but trust him to be behind one of the most bizarre things that has ever happened to me in a professional Premier League football match. Though I never did get to taste how good the burger was. Maybe next time, big lad!

I really enjoyed my time with Drogheda. It was a much more professional set-up than my time in the Irish League, and we even reached the semi-final of the FAI Cup – though we lost after a replay – but in the summer of 1974 came one of the most horrific and heartbreaking moments of my life, and one that would ultimately lead to my transfer from the Drogheda team.

Back then, summer league football was really popular and, although professionals were barred from playing in it by the Irish Football Association, lots of us broke the rules. My Drogheda teammate Danny Trainor had asked me if I would play for his local team, Ardoyne Celtic, in the

Buncrana Cup in County Donegal and I agreed. A short time later, a guy from the Ballymoney summer league team asked if I'd play for them in the Hughes Cup summer competition, and if I could get any of my Drogheda teammates to turn out for them as well. Big Trainor loved a game of football and he didn't care if it was legal or illegal, so the minute I mentioned the Hughes Cup, he told me to count him in. Two of my other teammates also agreed to play – Geordie O'Halloran and Gerry Brammeld, who had joined Drogheda around the same time as me.

On the day of the match, 10 August 1974, the three lads came down from Belfast. We played the game on a very wet night at Cricket Park in Ballymoney town centre and, after the game was over, we decided to go for a quick beer. A good friend of mine, Jimmy Wilson, drove Danny and Gerry in his car and I followed behind with Geordie and two other friends – Paddy Dunlop and Joe McVicker – in mine. We were driving along the Garryduff Road in Ballymoney, when another car approached from the opposite direction and suddenly swung right into Jimmy's lane – it was virtually a head-on collision. There was what seemed like an explosion with a massive shower of sparks. I slammed on the brakes and Geordie, Paddy, Joe and I ran towards Jimmy's car. The silence was eerie and there was the smell of warm metal. Both cars were absolutely mangled and tangled together. Almost immediately, I could see that the elderly local couple in the other car were already dead. No one in Jimmy's car was moving either.

The police and ambulance services quickly arrived on the scene and asked us all to move back. It was dark and wet, and we all huddled together, hoping and praying for good news. I knew one of the policemen on the scene, and a short time later he came over to give us an update, 'Sorry Liam, but your big mate Danny Trainor who was the front seat passenger in Jimmy's car didn't make it either.' He also informed me that the driver – my friend Jimmy – and my other teammate Gerry Brammeld were both critical and had life-threatening injuries. I was numb at the news. Danny had been a big, strapping, muscular man and a fine example of a tough guy. I'd always felt he was indestructible, yet he'd been killed in a split second. I will never forget the sight of him being laid flat on the footpath at the side of the road then covered with a sheet. It was awful. I was heartbroken too about the elderly local couple. I knew them and their family well – they were very decent people and highly-respected in Ballymoney. Attending the three funerals was absolutely heartbreaking and seeing the family members who had been left behind is something I'll never forget. I'm still choked up now thinking about it.

Jimmy and Gerry were taken to the former Route Hospital in Ballymoney, the two of them fighting for their lives. Thankfully they both survived, although Jimmy ended up with a bad limp as his legs had been badly injured in the crash. Gerry made a remarkable recovery and, against all odds, returned to playing senior level football. I love them both dearly.

The crash was a major factor in my decision to leave Drogheda. I had so many good friends there, but it just wasn't going to be the same for me without big Danny Trainor.

Coleraine FC

Then, in October 1974, came another tragedy that made me rethink my place in the Drogheda team. The Troubles were showing no sign of abating and it took very little for things to tip over into civil disorder. But things came to a head for me personally when I got the news that Jimmy Hasty, a very good friend and a great footballer who had played for teams on both sides of the border, had been shot by a gunman as he made his way to work one morning. It was the final straw for me. My mum was still worried sick about me crossing the border at least twice a week and I knew that something had to change.

It seemed that Lady Luck was on my side once again when, not long after the accident, two of my good friends and former Coleraine FC greats, players Ivan Murray and Johnny McCurdy, approached me completely out of the blue and asked if I'd consider signing for Coleraine, my local team. I was surprised but I must admit I was interested. Coleraine manager Bertie Peacock had built a super side – they had just won the Irish League – and he planned to hand the reins to Ivan and Johnny.

When I told my mother about the offer, I could see the sheer relief on her face. So I gave Coleraine the thumbs up and they got in contact with Drogheda about the transfer. There had to be an agreement on the transfer fee, so Coleraine got my mum to send Drogheda a letter thanking them for all they had done for me but saying that she wanted to see me playing football back in Northern Ireland. Her letter definitely helped, and the transfer fee was subsequently agreed. In the end, the fee was paid by the Ballymoney branch of the Coleraine Supporters Club, thanks to the two main men there – Robert Anderson and Alan Quigg, two good people devoted to the club.

I said my farewells to the Drogheda players and staff – I was sorry to leave as they had always been more than good to me. Arthur 'Mousey' Brady and his wife, Joan, were really good friends of mine and, although they're both gone now, I am still very close to their family.

The move to Coleraine marked the start of yet another era in my career and, in many ways, was one of the most successful. The Coleraine team was a quality one with several locals forming the core of the side. The chairman, Jack Doherty, also happened to be a major building contractor and no sooner had I arrived than he asked me to give him a quotation for plumbing and heating two bungalows he was building on the Mountsandel Road in Coleraine. I won the contract; then, as he made plans to build dozens more, I won the contracts for those too. I've lost count of how many houses I worked on for Jack. He was one tough businessman, but perfectly fair. It was definitely Jack who put an arse in my trousers in those days, of that there is no doubt.

I was doing really well in business and, after a bad patch, things were looking up in my personal life too. Unfortunately, June and I had split up just after I started playing with Drogheda. We had married too young and we knew the break was the right thing for both of us but it was still sad and we had our two kids, Louise and Lawrence, to think about. Recently though, I had met Gillian and we thought we might have a future together. Our relationship had been a big factor in my decision to leave Drogheda.

I was right to trust my instincts because, more than forty years on, we're still happily married and have four grown-up children – Janice, Lynsey, William and Robert.

On the football front, things were really taking off at Coleraine and we won lots of games and trophies. We had a great line-up then: Vincent Magee in goals, Johnny McCurdy at right-back, Davy Jackson was centre-back, I was sweeper beside him, and Eugene McNutt was left-back. The centre-midfield two were Ivan Murray and Brian Jennings, and the front four were Terry Cochrane on the right, Michael Guy and Dessie Dickson up front, and Frankie Moffatt on the left wing. Johnny and Ivan were good managers – no bullshit, just facts and figures. They were also top-quality players themselves and knew the game inside out. No coaching badges were required back then, just a good knowledge of the game, and they both had that in abundance.

We had a fantastic season in 1975 with that line-up, making it all the way to the Irish Cup Final – though that was a tough experience. The Irish Cup Final was always played at Windsor Park, Linfield's home ground, but Coleraine had objected to the venue on the basis that it would give Linfield an unfair advantage. As a result, the final was played at Ballymena Showgrounds, a neutral venue roughly halfway between Coleraine and Belfast. Coleraine thought that was only fair, but some Linfield fans felt differently and boycotted the match. It made headline news.

The game ended in a draw and for all important games back then, that meant a replay. The second game again took place at Ballymena and this time most of the Linfield 'stayaway' fans returned. Incredibly, the replay also ended in a draw, so we met in Ballymena once more. Linfield were a helluva team then, packed with quality players, and they were hard to beat but in the third and final game, we got the better of them by the narrowest of margins, with a score of 1–0, thanks to a goal by Jim 'Chang' Smith.

The vast majority of Linfield fans applauded as we attempted a victory lap of the pitch with the cup. Sadly, however, a few began to stone us and our lap of honour had to be cut short. I'll never forget the sound as some fairly large stones actually struck the Irish Cup trophy. I was especially disappointed as I had supported Linfield as a kid, as had many of my family, but such is life, and such is football. Most clubs have a few idiots who are hell-bent on spoiling it for everyone else. Incidentally, a couple of years ago I had an opportunity to get my hands on that old Irish Cup once again when I was invited to the Belfast Celtic museum in Belfast. I was able to point out to my hosts three or four fairly severe dents that I think were the result of it being hit by those stones.

After the match, we all got showered and changed before making our way to the team bus outside the stadium. A big crowd was still assembled outside, mostly waiting to see the players and, although Linfield had lost, there were still a considerable number of Blues supporters there as well. We had been chatting for a while with the supporters from both clubs, signing autographs and having pictures taken, when I saw a young girl, probably about nine or ten years of age, making her way towards me. She was wearing a Linfield scarf and holding an autograph book. Suddenly, the man she was with – it later transpired he was her dad –

pulled her back from me. I thought it strange, but we'd just won the Irish Cup and I was euphoric, so I didn't think any more about it. However, about ten or fifteen minutes later she appeared in front of me again, holding out her autograph book to be signed. Just as I went to take it, the dad said to me, 'Liam, I know you're a Prod, so could you please sign your name "Billy Beckett"? I don't want a Liam in her book.' I wanted to refuse and tell him where to go, but the wee girl was a lovely kid and I knew she'd be sad if I said no, so for the first and only time in my life I signed my name as 'Billy Beckett'.

A couple of years later, I was waiting for a friend on Royal Avenue in Belfast and a woman who was standing beside me said, 'I think that bus driver is shouting at you.' I turned around and there was this bus driver waving at me and shouting, 'All right, Billy?' Finally, the penny dropped – it was the same man and the wee shit was still calling me 'Billy'.

Two years later, in what was probably my most memorable domestic game for Coleraine, we found ourselves in the 1977 Irish Cup final against Linfield at The Oval in Belfast. The brilliant team we had in 1975 had begun to break up: Johnny McCurdy had retired, Ivan Murray was about to do the same and Terry Cochrane had been transferred to an English club. They were the elite – ranked among the top six players in the entire league – so, with all due respect, the players who replaced them just could not compare. We were up against a bloody good Linfield team and they were hot favourites to win. I remember their player–manager Roy Coyle had made a fairly rash statement to the local press on the morning of the final – something like, 'It could be 5' – and I wasn't confident that we had what it took to beat them. We had two or three weaknesses and the wily Coyle would make sure his team exploited our shortcomings to the full.

A huge crowd turned out to the stadium that day – my mum and family were all there, as were the families of most of the players. I remember thinking that we needed to start well and get possession of the ball, otherwise Linfield would have us chasing shadows. It was a really sunny day and, in the heat, we'd soon tire and be very vulnerable. Coyle was renowned as the 'hard man' in the centre of midfield for Linfield but, if the going got tough, we had Brian Jennings in there and he was no mug either – he knew how to take care of himself.

Being a defender, I never scored many goals, but I'd saved one for the final. We'd won a corner kick in the first half and, occasionally, if the opportunity arose, I would push forward for 'set pieces', just on the off chance that I might get on the end of something. On this occasion I saw that Linfield had left quite a lot of space outside their penalty area for our corner kick, which was being taken by Frankie Moffatt. I advanced forward into that free space and Frankie spotted me. He rolled the perfect short corner right into my path and, although I didn't connect properly, I got the shot away and it beat the Linfield goalie, Ken Barclay, at the near post. Once I heard the roar I knew it was in the net and we were 1–0 up. It maybe wasn't the most spectacular of goals, but it was a crucial one as it gave us confidence to take the game to Linfield.

A short time later, Jim Lemon scored an equaliser for Linfield and, when the half-time whistle came, the game was deadlocked at 1–1. But in the second half we started well and we went on to score three excellent goals through Dessie Dickson, Frankie Moffatt and Michael Guy, and when the final whistle sounded, we were comfortable 4–1 winners. Never in my wildest dreams did I think we would beat Linfield by such a comprehensive margin, especially since Coleraine were a much weaker team than the one we'd had in 1975.

I met my mum and family outside the dressing room, and gave them my medal and Cup Final jersey, but I wasn't going home just yet. The club had big plans to hold a mega celebration back at the Coleraine Social Club and the team were expected there around 8 p.m., so there was enough time for us to get a post-match meal on our way home. But the Ballymoney contingent of the team had different ideas. After the meal, we pleaded with our chairman, Jack Doherty, to let us off in 'the toon' on the way through to Coleraine so we could have a pint with our mates in our local pub, Gillans. It took a lot of persuading but finally Jack agreed, provided we only had the one and then immediately made our way to the social club to meet up with the rest of the team – that was the deal.

Alas, we never made it to the big celebration party. My family told me that they'd waited inside the packed social club as the team were called up to the stage one by one. The fans were going wild. But when they announced the four Ballymoney players – me, Dessie Dickson, Johnny McCurdy and Ivan Murray – we were nowhere to be seen. The truth was we were all 'half winged' and so merry by that stage that we had stayed in Gillans until we were all completely blootered. I don't remember an awful lot about it, but around 1 a.m., I must have decided I needed to go home.

I sneaked out the back over a wall into an old, reportedly haunted, graveyard, which is next to the pub. I somehow weaved my way through the headstones until I got to the large steel gates, which, to my misfortune, were chained shut. I gave them a good shake, as you do, to make sure they were definitely locked. Unbeknownst to me, a local man that I know well was walking past with his wee dog just at that moment. He let out an enormous squeal, dropped the dog lead and ran off down Queen Street. I still rib him about it to this day and he always says, 'Beckett, if I'd had a gun, I would have shot ye'. Had I not been blind drunk, there is no way I'd have been in that old haunted graveyard either. Every time I drive past it, I still get the willies.

I spent the rest of that night and the next day being sick, trying to comfort myself with the fact that it wasn't surprising I'd overdone it – it's not every day that you win the most prestigious knockout cup competition in local football for the second time. It was a dream come true.

I had given my mum both of the jerseys I had worn when we won the two Irish Cups and she had them washed and ironed and sitting folded in pride of place in her china cabinet in Ballymoney. Irish Cup final shirts are one-off jerseys that are specially designed: the cup, the names of the two finalists and the date are all embroidered on the left breast of the jersey. They are special mementos for the players to keep.

They were my mother's pride and joy and she protected them like they were the crown jewels. So one of my biggest footballing regrets is that I gave them both away. A work colleague of mine from the building site – he drove a JCB digger – was a big Coleraine fan. His family were fans too and he asked me if there was any chance that one of his sons, who had a fairly severe type of muscle-wasting disease and was in a wheelchair, could get a picture taken in a proper photographic studio with me and the Irish Cup. Of course I agreed – I was happy to do that – and he asked if I could possibly get his son an old Coleraine jersey to wear in the picture. Again, it would have been no problem for me to get a team shirt from the club but, typically, I forgot to collect it and, on the day of the photo shoot, I nipped to my mum's house and had to practically plead with her to let me borrow one of my Irish Cup-winning jerseys for the lad to wear in the picture. She turned me down point blank at first but came round when I explained the situation.

So off I went to the photographer's studio in Coleraine with the Irish Cup in one hand and my cup final jersey in the other. The lad and his dad were speechless when they realised he was going to get to wear the actual cup-winning jersey and it was lovely to see the joy on the boy's face.

After the photo was taken, and while we were still in the studio, the dad turned to me and said, 'Liam, is there any way you would consider selling that jersey? If so, I would try and buy it for my son.'

I said, 'Sorry, but no way.' I knew my mother would be sitting back in Ballymoney patiently waiting on its safe return.

'I would break the bank if you would put a price on it,' he told me.

I took one look at his young lad, who was still wearing the shirt and clearly reluctant to take it off, and saw how happy he was. 'You know what,' I said, 'that jersey fits you perfectly, young fella, and I think you should keep it.'

His father looked at me in disbelief. 'Liam, you still haven't told me the price. I maybe can't afford it.'

'You owe me nothing,' I told him. 'It's on me, he can have it for free.'

The journey home to Ballymoney, which normally takes about fifteen minutes, felt like hours. I was thinking, what the hell am I going to tell Mum? She'll be devastated. But I should have known better. My mum had a heart the size of Rathlin Island and, although she was shocked when I broke the news, she turned to me with tears in her eyes and said, 'Well done, son. I'm proud of ye.'

So that left only one Irish Cup-winning shirt in my mum's china cabinet and later it went a similar way when I gave it to a young fan with a serious illness. I just felt those kids needed them more than I did. However, I often wish I still had them to give them to my own kids – they'd be something to look back on when I'm no longer here – but that's life. Sometimes things have a way of working out, so you never know, maybe they'll come back to me and my family eventually.

Coleraine was a great team, especially the 1975 line-up, and as good, if not better, than any of the others in the Irish League, and the results and trophies we won backed that up. We won the City Cup, the Ulster Cup, the Gold Cup, and two Irish Cups, and this was at a time when both Linfield and Glentoran were very strong teams. We were regulars in Europe as well.

One memorable European game was when Coleraine were drawn against German champions Eintracht Frankfurt in the European Cup Winners Cup in 1975. Their team was packed with world-class players, many of whom were top internationals as well. We stood a better chance of getting struck by lightning than we did of getting a result against such a slick world-class outfit, so it was more of a damage-limitation exercise than a real match.

We arrived in Frankfurt to a massive stadium and a massive crowd and it was a backs-to-the-wall job for practically all of the game. We barely got a chance to venture anywhere near the German goal all night, such was their dominance, but Terry Cochrane – a real talent and a good lad as well – was still part of our team at that time and on his night he was as good as anyone the Germans had. In a flash of sheer brilliance, he scored a wonderful goal. He picked the ball up around the halfway line and ran at the Germans, beating a couple of their world-class defenders before slipping the ball into the back of the Eintracht net. It was a wonderful individual goal and one that definitely ruffled the feathers of the German players.

After that, the Germans attacked us with all guns blazing. It was like the Alamo: a non-stop onslaught. We were pounded by attack after attack to such an extent that at one point I shouted out, 'Who the fuck is hiding?' Midfielder Brian Jennings came back, 'We've only ten players, Becks, count them.' I did a quick headcount and it was true. Then Brian shouted back to me, 'It's TC. He's gone missing.' When I looked around, I was stunned to see Terry running up and down the running track that adjoined the pitch. He seemed to be stopping to talk to anyone and everyone.

I asked him what the hell he was doing and demanded he get back on the pitch. It turned out that, when he had scored his wonder goal for us, the stadium scoreboard had credited the Coleraine goal to 'Simpson' and not 'Cochrane'. Terry was both stunned and furious and had gone to find the scoreboard operator to get the name changed! To go walkabout during a European Champions League game must go down in history as a one-off and I still rib TC about it any time I see him. I didn't find it funny at the time, mind you.

The rest of the game passed without incident and, to be honest, we played really well to keep the score at 5–1 to the Germans at full-time. Yes, it was a defeat but it was considered a moral victory by many of the press corps afterwards.

Probably my best European result was in 1977/78, when Coleraine played an away game against the crack East German club, FC Lokomotive Leipzig, though the journey to the match was almost as much of an ordeal as the game itself. The first leg wasn't so bad: we flew from Belfast into West Berlin, were picked up by a luxury glass-topped coach and transported to the famous Checkpoint Charlie. Once there, however, we all had to disembark and make the border crossing on foot. The bus driver informed us that someone had been shot dead that very day trying to escape from East to West.

The border crossing was a wide, flat area with high wire fences that were dotted with signs warning us about landmines. The place was crawling with soldiers trained to shoot anyone trying to cross the border illegally. As we made our way through the designated passport and visa-control section, the soldiers not only checked all our ID documentation and personal baggage, they also insisted that our kit man empty all the team kit on to the ground, including our very football boots, where they went through everything with a fine-tooth comb.

Once the border guards were satisfied, we were all escorted to another bus on the eastern side. It was like an old workers' bus with wooden seats and practically no suspension. It was surreal in comparison to what we'd had in West Berlin. As we were boarding, we were all given a brown paper bag that contained a sandwich, apple and a small bottle of lemonade. It took me back to my Sunday school trips to Portrush when I was a kid.

As we drove the three hours to Leipzig, I could really see how different East and West were – it was like day and night. West Berlin was full of fast cars and flashing lights, but East Berlin was dark, bleak and years behind the West in terms of technology and luxury goods. The food was dreadful and the hotel we were staying in was old and dated. I can clearly remember looking out of my bedroom window the first morning we were there and seeing some women walking towards a building site just up the street. On their shoulders they carried wooden planks that, it turned out, were being used for scaffolding. Even Northern Ireland used modern metal tubular scaffolding, but not Leipzig.

One area in which the East Germans invested heavily, however, was sport. Bruno-Plache-Stadion was a real sight to behold. We were taken there on our first full day in Leipzig and, though there were no spectators, the stadium was buzzing. There was music playing and on the running track that surrounded the playing pitch were some very young children who had been identified as potential Olympic champions in track and field. These kids would regularly be taken out of school and brought to the stadium for coaching. It was then that I realised just why the East Germans were so successful at the Olympic games – it was an incredible spectacle to watch.

We trained on the stadium pitch that day and then did a little sightseeing before we returned to the hotel to relax. The game was scheduled for the following evening. The Lokomotive Leipzig team was packed with East German internationals, so we knew that as part-time professionals we would really be up against it.

On match day, the game had barely started when the Germans got a free kick about thirty yards out from our goal. The Leipzig inside-forward – nicknamed 'Dr Hammer' because of his lethal left foot – was up to take the shot so we built a wall of bodies to try and block off as much of the goal as humanly possible. Dr Hammer struck a shot over our heads and all I heard was a massive roar. The ball had smacked our crossbar – the entire set of goal posts must still have been shaking five minutes later.

That day ended in a 2–2 draw – probably the best European performance in which I've ever been involved. We'd battled really hard and deserved to get a share of the spoils but so irate were the Leipzig fans that their team of international superstars couldn't beat little old Coleraine from Northern Ireland, that once the final whistle sounded some of them pulled the blue plastic seats from their bases and fired them on to the pitch. That in itself told us that we'd done well. Then it was time for home and a repeat of the journey back through Checkpoint Charlie.

In hindsight, it was one of my most enjoyable experiences of playing football abroad, though as usual I was glad to get home to Northern Ireland. I'm a very plain eater and boy had I been looking forward to a bowl of homemade porridge.

Sadly, the next few years proved difficult for me and for Coleraine FC – I suppose all good things come to an end. The team at that time were in transition and quite a few of the players from the great sides of the early and mid-seventies had either left or retired. Truth be told, I was losing interest as well. The good times when we'd won everything were becoming but a distant memory.

Things didn't get any better for me when, in 1978, Coleraine appointed their former goalie and club stalwart Victor Hunter as manager. I had nothing but the highest respect for Victor – and he's still a really good friend of mine – but we didn't always see eye to eye on football matters. I felt Victor was signing far too many average players and I let him know it on a number of occasions. One night at training in early 1979 things came to a head and we had a heated exchange of words that resulted in me being placed on the transfer list by mutual consent. We were both headstrong and as stubborn as they come, and neither of us was prepared to give an inch – a transfer seemed the only way forward. Almost immediately, the papers were full of the news and Crusaders FC came in with an offer straightaway. The next day, I had a meeting with Crusaders chairman Derek Wade and manager Ian Russell. The club had met Coleraine's valuation and I'd agreed terms, which included a considerable signing on fee plus two new pair of football boots. We signed the necessary transfer forms there and then, enabling me to play that Saturday for Crusaders against Glentoran.

I found a much-changed dressing room of players at Seaview – a lot of the players I'd previously won the league with at Crusaders had moved on – and although manager Ian Russell was a lovely man, I got the feeling that I'd made a wrong move. I wasn't totally convinced that under this manager I could give as much as I had done in my previous successful spell with the club. There was much I could do about it, though – I'd made my bed, as they say. However, the entire transfer procedure took another incredible turn when the Coleraine chairman (and a great friend of mine) Jack Doherty retuned home from his holidays in America. He practically flipped when he heard what had happened and got straight on the phone to me and gave me a right bollocking. 'What the hell are you playing at?' he demanded. 'Your place is at Coleraine and nowhere else.' I must admit at that particular moment in time I reckoned he was pretty much spot on.

We talked things through and I agreed I'd come back to Coleraine. Jack immediately contacted Crusaders and was able to reverse the transfer. The uncashed cheque for the signing-on fee and the two new pairs of football boots went back to the Crues, along with an unreserved apology from me because I really liked the people at Seaview. I then re-signed for Coleraine. My whirlwind transfer had lasted a mere nine days – the shortest ever transfer in Irish League football history back then.

Back at Coleraine, I continued to be plagued by an ongoing groin injury. Senior football matches and the associated training are intense, and they put your body through the wringer. The experts told me that the best cure for my groin injury was rest, but I always tried to play though the pain.

Doctor Love – sadly passed away now – was the club doctor back then, and what a colourful, charismatic man he was. A few hours before each game he would give me a rather large painkilling injection into the injured area. It worked as a stop-gap measure, but the day after the game my groin would always be extremely sore.

The physio at Coleraine would also apply a liberal amount of Deep Heat ointment to the affected area before each game and, more often than not, it would come into contact with my genitals. Believe me, that brought true meaning to the phrase 'great balls of fire' and many a half and full time saw me searching for ice packs in the dressing room. It also ensured that I played each game with a fairly pronounced hearty glow on my face.

Coleraine also often sent me to former Glentoran and Northern Ireland trainer, Bobby McGregor, for treatment. Bobby was widely regarded as the best physio in the business, and was one of life's gentlemen, but he never took money for his services – not from me, the club, or, I'm led to believe, from any of the other Irish League players he treated. I couldn't have that, so I always stopped in at my local butchers in Ballymoney and bought him a parcel of sausages, streaky bacon, and so on. At the end of every session, he would say, 'Now go home and rest that, young Beckett,' but he knew damn well I'd be playing on the Saturday.

I suppose I didn't help myself much, but I loved the game – most players back then were the same and just played through the pain barrier. Nowadays, some players pull out of a game if they sneeze, in case they are taking a cold. But I couldn't deny that the injury was taking its toll and it had me considering whether it was time to walk away.

Then, in 1979, came the final straw. Coleraine had signed former Leicester City player, Gerry McGowan. In February 1979 McGowan was arrested over his alleged part in the shooting of a British Army soldier in Londonderry. McGowan signed a confession and was released on bail. He made his debut for Coleraine on 29 March 1979 and continued to play for them until February 1980. Many of my family were or had been members of the security forces so it was completely against my principles to play, train or even be associated with anyone linked to a paramilitary organisation, republican or loyalist. It was simply a non-runner. The club did their best to get me to stay, offering me a four-figure signing-on fee if I remained, but my mind was made up.

Shortly after my departure, the McGowan story took an unexpected turn. McGowan went 'on the run' and spent almost twenty years south of the border. He did resurface eventually and, in 1998, fought his case in the courts and was acquitted of any wrongdoing. It turned out that his confession had been forced. Not surprisingly, that confession went a long way to confirming McGowan's guilt for me back in 1979. My behaviour is a matter of some regret to me now, given that he was, in fact, innocent all along.

I was sorry that my last experience in Coleraine FC was such an upsetting one. I had been so happy there and had had so many fantastic teammates. But the decision had been made and that was it. My professional playing days were over. I was not sorry to wave goodbye to wet and windy nights on the mud heap of a training ground that was the Coleraine 'Wee' Showgrounds pitch but after a few weeks of home comforts, I did miss the weekly discipline, craic and team camaraderie. There was, however, no going back. The whistle had blown for the final time on my playing career.

From player to manager

My retirement from football in August 1980 gave me a chance for a well-earned rest and I was happy to have more time to spend with my family and on my plumbing business. It also gave me more time for my other sporting passion, road racing. I was able to get to a lot more races and from 1988 onwards I was working closely with Robert Dunlop. But I still had that passion for football burning inside me. So, when Ballymoney United FC, my local B Division club, came looking for me in 2000 to be their manager I knew it was a good way to get back into the game.

Ballymoney United were in pretty dire straits when I first arrived, but I had plenty of good contacts and I quickly put them to full use. I signed as many good local players as I could – those who weren't playing senior football – and we soon began to climb the table. By 2004, the team were playing superbly: we were in the top six of the league, with games in hand, and we were due to play in two major cup semi-finals.

I was riding high, proud of how well we were doing, when things came to an abrupt end in the club. We had just played an away game against Ballyclare Comrades and had headed into Ballymoney United Social Club for a pint before we all went our separate ways. I had my youngest daughter Lynsey with me. We had just sat down when one of the club committee – a complete arsehole and someone I never had any respect for – said something to me like, 'The rest in here might be scared of you, but I'm not.' It was a bizarre thing to say but, to be honest, I think that things are often not straightforward when you're on your own turf and when it's your own local club. People want you to do well, but not too well. There was probably something of that at the back of the comment. Not to mention that he'd had quite a few beers that day. He was a big lad and was leaning over me in an intimidating fashion when he was spouting off, so I stood up and smacked him. As I always knew, he was gutless, and that was the end of things, but I was pretty sure there and then that my time at the club was up. It's a pity, in my opinion, that the club hadn't a better committee at the time because Ballymoney was always a hotbed for good footballers and this team could have gone on to much bigger and better things. Alas, over the last few years they have gone the other way and are now playing junior football in the Ballymena and District League.

After my departure most of the Ballymoney team informed me they wanted to strike as a show of support for me but I told them to go and play for themselves, to play for their own pride, even if they no longer wanted to play for the club and intended leaving at the end of the season. Most of them did just that and then went their different ways.

A few days later I got a call from Moyola Park FC, another B Division club, but one with a great management infrastructure and a very hard-working and progressive club committee. The team had had a disappointing season and were looking for a new manager. I told them I was interested, and they asked if they could send a delegation from the club committee to come and see me at home that evening. About five or six of the committee turned up and we struck a deal then and there. It was clear that there was some urgency to my appointment. The club was at serious risk of relegation and my remit was a simple one: to ensure they stayed in B Division. It was a tall order as we only had a few games left to gain enough points to keep us safe.

The first thing I did was to change the training routine. I introduced an extra night of training a week, but I also brought in some fun training games that helped to lift morale. The art of being able to put a smile on players' faces shouldn't be underestimated. The feel-good factor that I created during training stayed with the team on the pitch and helped the players rediscover their self-belief. And, along with hard work and focus, it helped us get the results we needed to stay in B Division. Mission accomplished.

Cliftonville FC

A few months later, during the close season, I was contacted by Cliftonville FC, who wanted to talk to me about becoming their new manager. The Reds had just finished a poor season and, in fact, had only retained their Premiership status by virtue of relegation/promotion play-offs. What I'd achieved at Ballymoney United and

Moyola Park had obviously not gone unnoticed. It wasn't for nothing that I became known as 'Red Adair' after the American oil-well firefighter who built his reputation on being able to extinguish hazardous blowouts and fires – I always seemed to be called on to try and rescue teams that were in trouble.

I explained that, although I wasn't on a written contract with Moyola Park, I had given them a verbal assurance that I would be their manager for the new season. Nevertheless, Cliftonville still wanted to meet me and we agreed on the Adair Arms Hotel in Ballymena, halfway between Ballymoney and Belfast, in the hope that we'd be able to keep our meeting private and low key. The media were already beginning to speculate about my relationship with Cliftonville and the last thing we wanted was to have our meeting plastered all over the newspapers.

When I got to the Adair Arms, a four-man delegation from Cliftonville was waiting for me. No sooner had I set my arse on the seat than one of the hotel staff, who was a big football fan, came over and said, 'Well, Liam, what brings you to this neck of the woods?' My cover was blown. We decided not to take any more chances – the Cliftonville chairman asked for us to be moved to a private room immediately and we were soon ushered upstairs to a meeting room. The Reds committee made it quite clear that they wanted me as team manager and, to be honest, I was quite humbled that a Premiership team thought so highly of me at such an early stage in my management career.

Of course, I still had a verbal commitment to Moyola Park, but the Cliftonville director of team affairs assured me that he would smooth things over with the Moyola chairman. I was leaving the next day on a family holiday to Spain and I asked the Cliftonville board to give me a few days to think things over.

As well as my commitment to Moyola, I couldn't deny that taking a position with a predominantly nationalist club – Cliftonville are situated in a staunchly Catholic area of north Belfast – had me a little concerned. Not that it bothered me on a personal level – in fact, I think religion and politics should always be kept out of sports – but I still had to consider the effect that taking the job would have on the rest of my family and my friends. It would cause quite a few raised eyebrows in the unionist community, particularly in my hometown of Ballymoney. On the other hand, Cliftonville knew I was Protestant and were still prepared to employ me as their new gaffer – that sent the right message to me. I just needed time to think.

I was only on the second day of my Spanish holiday when Cliftonville phoned me to say that already there had been lots of speculation in the Northern Ireland newspapers that I was the hot favourite to be the new Reds boss and they were being inundated with requests to deny or confirm. They were wondering if I could give them my answer any sooner. I told them to give me a couple of hours and I would get back to them.

So I rang a few friends in Ballymoney to gauge what the reaction would be if I took the job. I didn't want any snide comments made to me or my family down the line. But the reaction was universally positive – everyone I spoke to told me to go for it and that I could be sure of their full support. So I got back to the Cliftonville chairman and told him he had a deal. For the remainder of my holiday my phone was red hot with calls from everyone and anyone. It was absolutely hectic.

The Cliftonville job was a big one as I had inherited a poor side. The fact that they'd only retained their Premiership status by the skin of their teeth was proof of that. I knew from the outset that I'd have to initiate a major rebuild. I was fortunate in that the team had some good pros like Keith Mulvenna, George McMullan, Liam Fleming, Declan O'Hara, and so on – good lads who really bought in to what we needed to do. They were the foundation on which I built the team and I'll never forget them for their support and trust. But the knack in managing a so-called smaller club is being able to identify a player that you know you can make better. That's exactly what I did at Cliftonville. I moved a tired player called Keith Mulvenna from a busy midfield role into a central defence role where the same mileage per game wasn't required and he was absolutely superb. I also released some of the club's more established players, the ones that I felt had passed their sell-by date and whose 'legs had gone', as they say in the game.

I then had to secure some new players. The player budget was very tight, however, so I knew I'd have to shop around – player recruitment had to be from either the lower leagues or from bigger clubs where decent players were surplus to requirements: lads who were available on a free transfer. To build a team with senior, experienced players is very often only a short-term fix, and can be an expensive one at that. It's vital to continue to blood youth if it's long-term success the club wants.

I found a great left-winger called Sean Friars at Finn Harps FC – what a talent he proved to be. I also found a young striker called Conor Downey languishing in Distillery seconds and, after one night's training, I knew he would make a super centre midfield player – later, the club sold him to Linfield for thousands. I also nailed the signature of a striker called Chris Scannell – a dentist who was coming back home to Northern Ireland to settle for good – who went on to become a Cliftonville legend. Though that particular signing was not without incident.

We were doing some pre-season training at The Dub, a big park up at the Mary Peters track in Belfast. I had arranged for Chris to meet me there while my first-team coach Eddie Patterson took the first-team squad away on a tough cross-country run. Chris arrived and, as we stood under a big oak tree in the park – me doing my best to get him to sign and trying to sell the club and my plans to him – a little white van pulled up and the guy rolled down the window. 'You haven't seen a football team called Cliftonville running around up here, have you?' I was somewhat taken aback and before I admitted to being the manager, I thought I'd ask him why he was enquiring.

'They come up here twice a week but they never book the facility and they never pay a penny.'

I was totally gobsmacked, but said, 'No, sorry, I haven't seen them, but I'll keep an eye out for ye.'

'Thanks,' he replied, and drove off.

I took one look at Chris and he was in fits of laughter. 'Are you sure you can pay me £80 a week, Liam?' he asked. Once my face had cooled a bit – it was as red as a baboon's arse – we got back down to business, and I finally got the thumbs up. Chris signed on a two-year deal and what a signing he proved to be – a great striker and a great fella as well.

The team really improved, and the new young players all settled down and gave a really good account of themselves. A happy, contented team always has a chance of succeeding and I was more than happy with our progress.

During my managerial career, there were three games that really stood out for me. One of them was during my time with Cliftonville. It was the opening tournament of the new season, the CIS Cup. We'd knocked the mighty Glentoran out in the quarter-finals and then drew the equally mighty Linfield in the semi-finals. The game was an evening kick-off under the lights at a neutral venue – The Oval in Belfast – and it was the biggest game that Cliftonville had played for a considerable period of time. Our wee team was flying and we were leading 1–0 as we went into added-on time at the end of the game. Our kit man was actually gathering up our gear in the dugout, ready for the final whistle, the final was beckoning and we were all on a high. It was a fantastic achievement for what had been a struggling Cliftonville team.

Suddenly Linfield punted a high ball into our penalty area. It was virtually the last kick of the game and our goalie – who I'd got on loan from a Dublin club as our normal keeper, Paul Straney, had been suspended – inexplicably dropped what was a simple catch right at the feet of the top Linfield marksman Peter Thompson, who tapped it into an empty net. The Linfield team and fans went ballistic while my Cliftonville players slumped to their knees on the pitch. A remarkable victory and cup final place had been snatched from us right at the death and we were all devastated. Now, somehow, we had to muster the energy and morale for an extra-time period of thirty minutes.

My young lads were mentally and physically shattered and another error by our goalie gifted Linfield the winning goal in extra time. We had been so, so close to reaching a major final, in what was only my very first year as a Premiership manager, yet two goalkeeping errors had cost us what would have been a massive and profitable occasion for the club.

Nevertheless, my spirits were lifted a couple of weeks later when I got the news that I'd been chosen as the Premiership manager of the month by the Football Writers Association. Obviously, I must've been doing something right!

In the end, I managed Cliftonville for just over a year and I want to go on record to say that, from the first day I walked in the front door of Solitude to the day I walked out for the last time, I was always made to feel welcome. The supporters were very good to me and the decent people at the club couldn't have done more. The Cliftonville chairman, Hugh McCartan, and most of the club committee were really lovely but, like most clubs, there were a couple of difficult people on board. Working with people like that is part and parcel of the job as a manager, and mostly I was able to get on with it. But in 2005, I identified a player that I wanted to sign and, for reasons I couldn't comprehend, a couple of the board members didn't want to sanction the signing.

I immediately resigned. If you are a manager and others deny you a signing you want to make, especially for reasons that I felt had nothing to do with football, then it's time to stick by your principles and move on. Gerard Lawlor, Cliftonville director of team affairs, actually came to Ballymoney to see if I would change my mind, but I knew I was making the right decision and so we parted company.

Thankfully, I still have many friends at Solitude and I'm glad of that because I really enjoyed my time there. Even the way things ended up hasn't taken the shine off. I still have a very warm relationship with the club.

Institute FC

Once word got out that I had finished up with Cliftonville, another Premiership club, Institute FC from Londonderry, contacted me about managing the team. They were also struggling to retain their Premiership status and so we agreed to talk.

I met chairman Raymond Smith in Portstewart on the north coast, and he made a first-class job of selling his club to me. I told him I was interested, and another meeting was hastily arranged, this time in a hotel on the outskirts of Londonderry with all the board members in attendance. I was impressed by the sheer warmth and decency shown to me by the club directors and it was during that meeting that they officially offered me the job. I came home to think it over, but it didn't take too long for me to accept.

On my very first night at the club as the new manager I addressed the players and staff at the club room. I spoke pretty slowly and clearly because sometimes my broad north Antrim accent is hard to understand, particularly when I am speaking quickly. I was about halfway through my maiden speech when I noticed that a few of the players, particularly the three from France and Belgium who were sitting at the back of the room, were looking a bit puzzled. 'Can you lads understand me?' I enquired. Just then, one of the local Derry lads in the team stood up and said, 'I would doubt it, Gaffer. Even we don't understand a word you're saying!' The room exploded in laughter. It was a great ice-breaker for me as a new manager. From then on, it was as if we'd all known each other a lifetime.

Unfortunately, Institute were in serious trouble. They had made a bold move and brought in the three players from France and Belgium. I realised very quickly that not only were these players not good enough but that the club quite simply couldn't afford them. It was a no-brainer – they had to go, and as quickly as possible. It was a shame because Institute were a small but well-run club. They liked to keep their house in order both on the pitch and off it, but in those signings they'd got their sums and strategy badly wrong. The club was in real danger of getting into serious debt.

It was Christmas 2005 when I took over the managerial reins and the players in question not only had contracts for the remainder of the season, but also for the season after that. I brought the three lads in individually to explain to them that the gamble the previous management team had taken hadn't paid off and that I'd have to let all three go to try and save the club from going under financially. However, they were having none of it and told me in no uncertain terms that they'd be going nowhere. They knew only too well that if the club wanted rid of them then the onus was on the club to pay up.

Ironically, the goalie, who was the best of the bunch,

was out with a long-term injury and I only used the other two players periodically as substitutes. Once the going got tough on the pitch these lads simply hadn't the heart for the fight – they were more the technically-gifted type than the big-hearted, physical type we needed just then. The club were in relegation trouble and the team was crying out for players who would roll up their sleeves and dig out the results we needed. With only a few games left and no funds to bring in any new players, the inevitable happened and the 'Stute' got relegated. I'd done all I could and tried my best, but we simply weren't good enough.

I'll never forget the night that relegation was confirmed. I stood outside our dressing room speaking with the press when I saw a large figure lurking in the dark, obviously waiting to speak to me. As the press people walked away, I suddenly realised that the person waiting was our skipper, David 'OG' Ogilby. Big David was an excellent player and a much-respected person around the club. 'Are you staying on, Gaffer?' he asked. 'If you're staying, then so am I.' David could have easily secured another Premiership club without any problem, but he was prepared to stay. That meant a lot to me. I told him I was going nowhere; I was staying on to try and get us back to the Premier League. I was lucky that several of my other top players, like Paddy McLaughlin, Kevin Ramsey, Declan Divin, Ruairi Boyle, and others, all wanted to remain as well. They were up for the challenge, and so was I.

The club finally managed to agree a severance package with the three foreign players and we also managed to offload some others who I didn't consider able for the fight that would take us back to the big time.

We started the 2006/07 season in the Championship but conducted ourselves with the same professionalism that we'd shown in the Premiership. We won the league for the first time ever in the club's history, by a clear seven points at the finish. We did the double by also winning the Carnegie Cup. I was delighted to be the first manager in the club's history to win the Championship title and, with it, the big prize of promotion back to the top tier of Irish League football.

Those victories were particularly sweet for us given all the pain of relegation and the hard work we'd had to put in to pick ourselves back up. The Carnegie Cup Final match took place in August 2006 and was against Belfast's Dundela FC. The match was played at a neutral venue – Stangmore Park in Dungannon. Institute's club committee had told me before the match that, if we won, it would be the biggest, most prestigious victory in the club's entire history, so the pressure was on. Dundela were a good side but that 'Stute' side I had back then were a class above. We won the final reasonably comfortably and I'll never forget the sheer joy on the fans' faces at the final whistle – quite a few had tears in their eyes. Everyone on the Institute board of directors was ecstatic – we had just landed the biggest trophy in the club's history. But the best was still to come.

The two biggest prizes in Championship One that season were the Carnegie Cup (which we had just won) and the League Championship – the biggest and most prestigious prize in any league in the world. It was the big one everyone wanted to win. The season was drawing to a close and Institute were top of the league and we found ourselves facing a tough game away against Harland

& Wolff Welders FC, a very good team. We knew that if we won that match, it would be mathematically impossible for any other team to catch us – we would be League Champions. The incentive to win that game couldn't have been bigger or better.

A big crowd was in attendance on the day of the match, and the stage was set. My job was to keep the players totally focused on the game itself and not let them get distracted by all the media hype, which had been cranking up the week before the game. But we needn't have worried – we played really well that day and won the game comfortably. The scenes immediately after the game were incredible and I was so proud. It was a special time for all of us at Institute.

We had won the League Championship for the first time ever in the club's history – by a clear seven points at the finish – and we'd done the League and Cup double. I was so proud. Most importantly, we were now back in the top tier of Irish League football.

In the summer of 2007, my contract was due for renewal and so the club arranged a meeting with me in the upstairs room of the 'Coffee Stop' in Drumahoe, Londonderry. The club were keen to extend my contract and I didn't need much persuading. However, my mum Maud was seriously ill and I made it clear that if her health worsened I would need to take time away from my role as manager to look after her. The club were very understanding and happy to proceed with the contract on that basis.

Shortly after the start of the new Premiership season, my mum's health deteriorated and she was hospitalised. Football took up so much of my time that my wife, Gillian, looked after Mum. She was with her 24/7 in hospital and

I knew that it wasn't fair on her, or on Mum. During one hospital visit, when I was sitting alone by Mum's bedside, I finally got it into my head that she wasn't going to get better. I finally accepted the fact that I needed to forget about football and be with her for whatever time she had left. It was a Tuesday, my usual training night, and when she asked me why I wasn't at the club, I told her that I'd taken the night off. Normally, she would have given me a right earful and told me, 'Get to your football, boy,' but for the first time ever she replied, 'Ah well, son, there'll be football when I won't be here.' I knew my mum was dying and I'm convinced she did too.

In March 2008, I told Institute that I would be leaving the club indefinitely – I knew I had been unable to focus on the team properly for a while – and I recommended my number two, John Gregg, as my replacement. John knew the players, he was a good coach and I reckoned the transition would be pretty smooth. So, John was appointed manager and did a very decent job in my eyes.

Mum clung to life for almost another six months before, in October 2008, she finally slipped away one evening in the Causeway Hospital in Coleraine. After she died, I completely lost my desire to go back into football management. Despite a few offers, I just couldn't muster the interest to return as a gaffer at any club. I still loved the game, and I was still immersed in that world – I had been doing some BBC punditry and had just started a weekly column for the Belfast *News Letter*. But while both commitments were time consuming, they did not take up as much of my time as football management had done.

Managing, my style

I became a manager because I loved the game and, after I had stopped playing, had still wanted to be involved in it. Looking back now, though, I can see that managing was a better fit for me. When you're a player, everything's done for you; when you're a manager, you're a motivator, a financial advisor, a therapist, a marriage guidance counsellor, and you have to be the boss. You're not one of the lads any more.

I hadn't found the transition that hard, to be honest, but then I was used to having responsibility. I'd been aware from a very young age that my mother needed me to do my bit. We were a tight-knit unit as a family, and we all needed to pull together to survive. I learned fast that you should never expect people to do things for you. You need to get up off your arse and do things for yourself.

I'd done my time as a player and I reckoned I knew how to get the best out of other people. I'd always, rightly or wrongly, had more respect for a manager who had played the game at a decent level – Irish League at the minimum. I'd resented being lectured by a manager who couldn't play the bloody game himself and I usually stared at the ceiling or floor during those types of team talks. I was happy in my own skin, confident and reasonably knowledgeable. A lot of players lack self-belief and focus – they always beat themselves up, thinking they weren't good enough, weren't playing well enough, or both. My job as manager was to give them confidence and encourage them to give 100 per cent to the team.

'Leave nothing in the tank,' I used to tell them. 'If you

give everything you have, then you can go to bed and fall asleep pretty quickly. If you feel you have cheated by not giving your all, then you'll twist and turn because of your conscience.' I was a great believer in everyone earning their keep – an honest day's work for an honest day's pay – and that was a two-way thing – they trusted me to do my bit and I trusted them to do theirs. That meant bringing some of them down from the clouds and getting other ones up off their arses.

As a player who becomes a manager, you bring all the good things that you've picked up from the managers that you've played under. The best are the ones you respect the most, the ones who had a unique way of getting the very best out of you as a player. One of my favourites, a man who taught me a lot, was my former Crusaders manager Billy Johnston. The dressing room could be a volatile place, where tensions spilled over. It was not unknown for a manager, frustrated by the performance of his team in the first half, to throw a cup or some other piece of crockery from the tray of refreshments set out for the half-time break. In fact, if things were particularly bad, the odd manager had been known to upend the whole tray in frustration. But that wasn't Billy's style. Although he was quite reserved, he didn't need to raise his voice to make us listen. I am a great believer in 'less is more' – very often, saying something short and focussed has more of an effect on the team than dragging it out and saying the same thing ten different ways. Billy was the master of that approach. He said very little but got the message across loud and clear: whatever he said always seemed to make sense and it stuck with us. I would have done anything for him.

Ivan Murray and Johnny McCurdy, the management duo at Coleraine, were also favourites of mine and had a big influence on me. They were a bit more vocal – and they did swear – but they also got the message across. No bullshit, just to the point, and certainly not the 'coaching-guru' type that you get nowadays. Again, I would have kicked the door down for them. This pair had built their footballing reputations on the quality of their playing rather than the quantity of their coaching qualifications – often a requirement today. Ivan and Johnny may have lacked in the theory side of the game but they more than made up for that with their practical experience. If I had to make a choice, I'd always opt for someone who has a wealth of practical experience. Both those men had excellent playing ability and a great tactical awareness – they were excellent managers and good lads as well.

No other manager ever got the best out of me like Billy, Ivan and Johnny did – they were the best managers I ever played for. They knew that strong mutual respect is needed between managers and players. They also knew that no two players are the same. Some need an arm around their shoulders at times, while others need an occasional boot up the hole. They taught me a lot, though I never really realised how tough being the gaffer was until I became one myself. It's tough as a manager to keep all the players happy.

'Total respect but no fear' had been my mantra and what I'd expected from all my players. I had a poster with those words up in the dressing rooms of all the teams I managed. Another favourite of mine, and something I used to say to the players when we were up against a team with a big reputation, was, 'Remember, it's not the size of the dog in the fight, it's the size of the fight in the dog.' Things were different back then. Successful teams were full of players that played with pride, and that kind of integrity shone through. Being in a team was about more than just the money. What mattered was the game itself and the prestige of winning – the money was secondary. Now it often seems as if it's the other way around.

The biggest challenge for me in the job was my temper. It had always been an issue really. When I first signed as a player for Coleraine, former manager Bertie Peacock had told me I was a 'crabbit shite', but it takes one to know one and Bertie suffered from a bit of a quick temper himself. He had played for Celtic for over ten years and told me he'd been given great advice by his old Celtic manager, Jock Stein: 'Count to ten. You do your team no favours whatsoever getting sent off, so count to ten and you'll see things differently.' For the first two matches after that, my behaviour was impeccable. Then, in the third game, a player from Portadown started to taunt me not long after kick-off. Obviously, his manager had told him to get under my skin because they knew my discipline was suspect. And they were right because I chinned him and got sent off. I sat in the dressing room on my own while the game was going on, full of remorse because I'd let my teammates down. After the game, Bertie, who had been among the spectators, asked me, 'What happened to counting to ten, son?' 'Sorry, Bertie,' I said, 'I only got to six.'

I was always really driven to win. Even losing a practice game at training annoyed me. And the pain of defeat stayed with me until the next game when I relished the chance to get back out and put things right. I very much saw myself as the protector of my players and that made for some problems. I had lots of verbal exchanges with managers from opposing teams, lots of verbal exchanges with fans. I got an awful lot of abuse from some fans when I was standing on the sidelines. Sometimes there would be people spitting over the fence at me or shouting personal abuse about my family. And when my team played in grounds where the fans were closer to the pitch, that was even harder to take. I had a path wore to the IFA disciplinary office.

Of course, the job had its downsides – during my managerial career I met a few people who didn't stand the knowing, a few arseholes who, once they pulled on a club blazer and tie, suddenly felt they knew it all – but I enjoyed virtually every minute of it.

It's all changed now, of course, and the job is much different to how it once was. I believe that a manager should have final say on all team affairs but that's no longer a widely-held view – player power seems to be the in thing and the manager has become little more than a puppet on a string. For me, that's wrong, and it's one of the main reasons why I could never return to the role with any club. I loved my time as manager, and I like to think I left every club I managed in a much better state than it was in when I arrived.

On air

Never in my wildest dreams did I envisage myself becoming a regular BBC sports pundit, or a sports columnist for one of the national weekly papers. With my broad north Antrim country accent and a standard secondary school education, I didn't have the ideal CV from which to launch a media career.

I had done a few radio and television interviews over the years through my involvement in football and the bikes, but I was always on the other side of the microphone or camera. In fact, I used to take awful stick from presenters, friends and family – they used to say that people would somehow need to get subtitles on their radios in order to understand my broad Ulster-Scots accent.

Around 2005, though, one man had enough trust and faith in me to use me as his sidekick in some of his radio shows – my old Crusaders teammate and now UTV and BBC presenter Jackie Fullerton. I must have done well enough because then I was asked by the BBC to do a bit of sports punditry on both football and road racing. I did spots on *Jackie's Christmas Cracker,* as well as on his BBC Friday night pre-North West chat show, and on Radio Ulster's *Sportsound* on a Saturday. Initially, I felt way out of my depth. I knew my education was limited and my grammar was not always perfect, but Jackie kept encouraging me, kept giving me the nod of approval. He was the consummate professional – he taught me to always do my homework before an event, irrespective of how big or small the event was. It didn't matter whether it was a Milk Cup youth football game or an Irish Cup final, he always insisted on perfection. 'Fail to prepare then prepare to fail' was Jackie's warning and that's still something I always have in mind. I think the listeners appreciated the fact that I had practical experience of many of the things I was talking about – I'd walked the walk – and that I brought a bit of humour to the proceedings. Sport is there to be enjoyed, after all.

I am also extremely fortunate to work with a superb producer in the BBC sports department called Brian Johnston. His attention to detail is meticulous and he never loses his warmth and calm assurance, regardless of the pressure we very often work under. I owe him a lot.

I work regularly with Joel Taggart and Michael McNamee, two commentators and presenters with very high standards. They have also been incredibly supportive and always inspire me to raise my game. They are only too ready to help in any way they can, and have taught me a lot – most of it good! The entire *Sportsound* team – not forgetting Grant Cameron, Michael Hammond, Eric White, and 'Mrs Fixit' Karen Elliot who is now retired – are a joy to work with, from the presenters to the sound engineers, as are the rest of the Sport NI team.

Mind you, we've had some adventures. Like the time Jackie, Joel and me were on commentary at a Donegal Celtic game against Linfield at Celtic's Suffolk Road stadium. The game had just started and we were in full-flight commentary when a man just in front of us threw himself backwards on to his seat. Such was the force of his action, he completely crashed through the back of his seat and landed on top of Jackie, who let out a squeal like a stuck pig. None of the rest of us could utter a word for laughing and the next few seconds of the game had virtually no commentary – there was silence on the airwaves as we tried our best to compose ourselves while Jackie moaned about his bruised legs and privates.

A similar incident happened to me and Joel when we commentated on a match between Cliftonville and Linfield at Solitude stadium. We were in the commentary booth, which, at Solitude, is situated in the middle of the upper deck of the old double-decker grandstand. Our seats are actually part of the spectator seating and, although there's a piece of tape to mark the area off, the fans are packed tightly all around us when it's a full house.

The stadium that day was packed to the rafters. Some people had clearly slipped into the upper deck of the double-decker stand without tickets, which meant there weren't enough seats for everyone – though, fair play to the Cliftonville stewards who made sure to clear anyone sitting on the steps or blocking corridors or pathways. However, there was one fan who had managed to gain entry without a ticket standing behind me on the steps. He was a fairly big lad and was heavily intoxicated, swaying considerably as a result of the alcohol. The stewards requested that he leave immediately but, as he attempted to step down towards the exit door, he lost his balance. The next thing I knew, he came crashing down into the commentary booth. He fell on to me first, sending my microphone and match notes flying through the air into the fans in front of us. My neck was bent forward, my chin jammed tight down against my chest. Such was the momentum of the big fella's fall that he crashed off me on to Joel, smashing the microphone off Joel's teeth. Miraculously, none of Joel's teeth were broken. The man finally came to rest jammed in at our feet and it took considerable time for the stewards to dislodge him and escort/carry him out of the ground. Thankfully none of us, including the big lad, were seriously injured, though we were all shaken.

Another very memorable occasion with Joel also happened at Solitude, again at a massive game between

Cliftonville and their bitter cross-city rivals Linfield. Linfield's fan base is mainly Protestant and Cliftonville's is mainly Catholic, and there's no love lost when the two sides meet. In fact, such was the bitterness between the two, that this particular fixture didn't take place for years – that it happens now is a measure of just how far we have come inn Irish League football.

The game that Joel and I were commentating on was a sell-out as Cliftonville had a chance of winning the league – we were completely surrounded by a sea of red-and-white clad Cliftonville fans. We were about ten minutes into the commentary when suddenly this guy arrived in front of us dressed as the Pope. He had it all – the cape, the wee hat, it was absolutely brilliant, and he even had an entourage of minders with him. It's no real secret that Joel and I are both Protestants, not that it should matter, but chances were that we were the only two Prods in the entire grandstand. Next thing we knew, the Pope began to publicly bless both of us. We were in fits and so were the hundreds of Reds fans who looked on. I actually said on air, 'My goodness, the Pope has arrived and he's late,' to which Joel replied, 'Ah well, we'll make allowances as he's come a fair way.' It was one of the funniest and most bizarre incidents we've ever had during live commentary.

It wasn't always fun and games, though. One time, Joel and I were commentating at an Irish Cup game – between Championship club Moyola Park and cup-holders Glenavon – played at the Castledawson home of the Intermediate club. The stadium didn't have a designated commentary booth at its compact ground so they'd erected scaffolding that elevated us about fifteen feet off the ground. Although it was of solid construction and well built, it wasn't much more than a flat wooden platform, and it had no sides or roof whatsoever – it offered us no protection from the elements, and the weather was absolutely Baltic.

Many other games that particular Saturday had been cancelled due to the icy conditions underfoot, but the Moyola ground has a 3G artificial pitch so match officials gave that game the go-ahead. No sooner had we begun commentary than it suddenly became very dark overhead and on came a very heavy shower of icy sleet and snow. Almost immediately, our match notes and stats were completely soaked and destroyed, and both of us were wet through.

We were wearing appropriate clothing for the conditions, but our gloves were made of wool so were soon soaking and, given the temperature had dropped to minus six, we soon felt like blocks of ice. We were both drenched and foundered before it even got to half-time, but we struggled on in the hope that some kind person might bring us a lovely warm cuppa, and someone from Moyola, a really hospitable club, duly obliged.

That revived us ever so slightly but, as the second half got going, the temperature began to plummet even further. Joel's face slowly took on a purple tinge and his lips were beginning to visibly freeze. He told me I was the same. Soon we were starting to slur our words and it was clear that we were in the early stages of hypothermia.

The match was deadlocked and, with only a few minutes left, extra time was a distinct possibility – but I doubt if Joel or I could have survived another half hour. Luckily, in the dying seconds of the game, Glenavon scored a winning goal and, even though Joel and I were completely neutral, I don't think either of us were ever as happy to see a team score.

We somehow managed to do our customary post-match summaries and then we walked like two cardboard cut-outs towards the warmth of the Moyola clubrooms. I can remember clearly the Glenavon manager's partner holding my hands for about fifteen minutes before I got any feeling back in my fingers. I've never endured anything like it, and at one stage during the second half I was genuinely concerned about Joel. If our bosses at the BBC had had any idea of the awful conditions we would experience that day, they would most definitely have pulled the commentary for our health's sake.

The game now

There is no doubt that the game I grew up knowing and loving has changed dramatically over recent years and I'm afraid much of it is not for the better. Admittedly, facilities have improved for spectators and players alike. Back in my day, spectators at the Railway Road end at my club Coleraine used to have to stand on exposed grassy slopes, and those kinds of conditions were not unusual for spectators at many other clubs. Now, there's concrete terracing and proper cover that gives protection from the elements at all grounds. As for the players, dressing rooms used to have a communal tub, which we all jumped into, with some players still wearing their boots. Showers were in very short supply. Training facilities too were primitive with poor lighting and poor surfaces. You wouldn't get that now – footballers today don't know they're living.

However, one of my major concerns is that nowadays the game is too money-driven. So many of the decisions in the sport revolve around the question, 'How much am I getting?' The salaries being shovelled out to many players are nothing short of obscene. We all like having an extra few quid in our pocket but there comes a time when you have to differentiate between what's fair and what's greed. This focus on money has, I feel, created a game that is riddled with prima donnas and players who dive to the ground, simulating serious injury when, in truth, they've received minimal, if any, contact whatsoever. Back in the day, it was a sign of weakness to go down injured in a football match unless you were seriously hurt; now it's the exact opposite.

The art of hard tackling has all but been removed from football as well – the modern game is nowhere near as physical as it once was. In many ways, I feel the game has sacrificed skill and ability for power and pace, and it hasn't made the game any better. The art of dribbling and the freedom to express natural skill has, to a certain extent, been replaced by systems and tactics. For example, I had a young player at Cliftonville who was tremendously skilful with the ball at his feet and blessed with the ability to skin a defender with ease. He was chosen to represent one of the Northern Ireland underage teams. On his return from international duty, he told me, to my surprise, that he hadn't really enjoyed it. The reason was that he'd been told by the international manager not to dribble with the ball in his own half but to pass it to a teammate. The manager's approach seemed to me wrong-headed in all kinds of ways. Not only did it fly in the face of what made this player special and what had caused him to be selected to play professional football in the first place, but it had also forced the young lad to play in a manner that was foreign to him, one that didn't come naturally to him or play to his strengths, and now he was demotivated and frustrated. This is an all too common story and it goes to the heart of a big concern of mine – the way in which many so-called coaching gurus bend the ears of the youngest kids at grassroots level. They over-coach the kids in terms of systems, tactics and patterns of play. I think this is totally wrong. Young kids just need a structured platform on which to enjoy the sport – they must be allowed freedom to get involved and enjoy the game. I hate to see coaches standing in the middle of a football pitch filling kids' heads with tactical nonsense. Just give them a ball and let them get on with it, for goodness' sake. There may come a time when those players need guidance on systems and tactical awareness, but not when they're just starting out. I know that many coaches do a wonderful job as volunteers but some of them can do more harm than good.

Football used to be one of the simplest games in the world. Now, sadly, it's become one of the most complicated, all because of over-the-top analysis – particularly on television. While some technological advances in the way we watch and experience football are welcome – replays, slow motion and additional cameras that show you goals from every angle are all helpful – some are not. Take Video Assistant Referees (VAR), for example. That's one form of modern technology that we don't need in football – healthy debate around the ref's decisions has always been vital part of the game. In addition, VAR has introduced more stoppages to a game that already has far too many stoppages, what with the current trend of divers and that stupid habit of kicking the ball out of play every time a player goes down 'injured'. VAR may well aid the referee but the final decision is still arrived at by a human being, so why not keep the game flowing by abiding by the initial decisions made on the pitch? It shouldn't matter whether that decision is a good or bad one. The focus should be on minimising stoppages and keeping the game flowing. To me this also means having fewer officials – four officials is more than adequate at all Irish League games.

And the powers-that-be would do well to stop meddling with the rules of the game too. When I think of the countless changes made to the offside law alone, for instance, it's abundantly clear that they are making a complete Horlicks of the game in terms of additions and rule changes. I shudder to think what the next fifty years will bring.

People say I'm old school because I believe matches are won or lost on the pitch. I'm not particularly interested in PowerPoint displays or people with laptops or high-tech simulations. It may be the modern way football is being played but, for me, it sucks a lot of the enjoyment out of the sport. If I'm watching a match at home, I don't switch on until three minutes before kick-off as the pre-match over-analysis bores me to tears. I'm scunnered before a ball's even been kicked.

The game itself is in danger of becoming much too predictable, with far too many manufactured players that have been coached to fit a manager's style of play. Football is now about patience and possession, with the

My all-time hero, Harry Gregg – we always have a laugh.

On my annual Black Santa sit-out at the Diamond in Ballymoney.

Darren Crawford

My mentor and long-time friend, Jackie Fullerton.

On official Harry Gregg Foundation duties with the man himself.

Me and John 'May McFettridge' Linehan.

Hosting a chat show with golfer Michael Hoey, rugby player Stephen Ferris and Northern Ireland football manager Michael O'Neill.

Prior to a chat show with some famous footballers –
(L–R), David Healy, Roy Carroll, Pat McGibbon and Neil Lennon.

Commissioning a new freshwater well in Burkina Faso in Africa with Drop Inn Ministries.

Met these budding footballers wearing a football kit I'd sent out
to Burkina Faso.

Receiveing my MBE at Buckingham Palace – my mum Maud
would have been so proud.

emphasis on keeping the ball at all costs. I've actually heard some commentators enthuse about a team having thirty consecutive passes. So what? They often haven't made it out of their own bloody half in the process. In years gone by the emphasis was on getting the ball up to the opponent's penalty area quickly and by whatever means possible, but the way the game is played now robs the fans of any of that excitement and drama.

I live in hope that one day some properly qualified person with practical experience will be installed at the top of our governing body and own up to the fact that enough is enough – otherwise football will soon bear no resemblance to the sport I've always loved.

Changing lives and building bridges

Harry Gregg was always one of my heroes. Even as a kid kicking a football up against the gable of our wee end-terrace house in Ballymoney, I looked up to him. He was the goalkeeper for the mighty Manchester United and for Northern Ireland, and even though I was an outfield player, he was my great inspiration. He came from a modest, working-class family and had overturned the odds to become a football star, despite facing more than his fair share of adversity as a child. Harry lived just a few miles down the road from me so he often appeared in the local newspapers and that gave the rest of us football-mad working-class lads hope that maybe one day we too could become professional footballers. He was living proof that getting to the very top in professional football was not impossible for young country lads from Northern Ireland.

Over the years, Harry has continued to grow in stature for me. Not only did the big man go on to be a proper legend – a word I use sparingly – in the game, he also became a national hero for his brave actions during the 1958 Munich air disaster, in which a plane carrying journalists, supporters and the Manchester United team crashed after take-off from a west German airport. Twenty-three people lost their lives in the disaster, but Harry had helped pull survivors from the wreckage.

Just as important to me, however, is the fact that despite all he achieved in football and all the adulation he continues to receive, he has never changed. So many other professional footballers become Big Time Charlies – once they've found success they forget where they came from and the friends who helped them get there. Harry is one of the exceptions to the rule: he has always remained grounded despite his incredible success. I am privileged to have had this colossus of local sport as a true friend for many years now.

I am also honoured to be a patron of the Harry Gregg Foundation, which was launched in 2014 to give kids from all backgrounds a chance to fulfil their dreams through participation in football, sports and other socially inclusive activities. In terms of football, it aims to give youngsters a solid, structured platform from which to enjoy a game of football without the fear of being over-coached by people who don't know any better. I agreed to be a patron because I know first-hand that football and sport can change lives – it changed mine. I'm very aware that it's all too easy now for kids to stay camped in their bedrooms playing on their phones or games consoles. Hand in hand with that, they are often eating rubbish – comfort eating, really – crisps and sweets and other junk. They're not getting out into the fresh air or getting enough exercise, and that isn't giving them a great start in life.

As we all know, obesity and mental health issues are on the rise among kids. Sports can help kids to avoid those issues or teach them how to cope with them better. That's why, in addition to being part of the Harry Gregg Foundation, I work with kids at a grassroots level by visiting schools and talking to groups of kids all over Northern Ireland. I want to try and pass on my love of sport, and particularly football, and try to encourage them to get out, get active and eat well. That's what sport's all about and I sometimes think we've forgotten that.

I have said it for years, and I will continue to say it for as long as I have breath in my body: sport is Northern Ireland's greatest common denominator. We've always been able to depend on sport to grab us global headlines for all the right reasons. For such a small country, we punch way above our weight in lots of sports and, for the size of our population, we have produced several European and World champions across a range of sporting disciplines. People like the Dunlops, Mary Peters, George Best, Carl Frampton, Barry McGuigan, Rory McIlroy, Jonathan Rea, Pat Jennings and so on have all been the glue that has united Northern Ireland through good times and bad. That is why I continually appeal to politicians to invest heavily in sport – it is this country's greatest asset.

PART THREE & ALL

In the papers

In 2005 *Ballymoney Times* editor Lyle McMullan approached me to ask if I'd be interested in writing a weekly strip column on football. I was managing Ballymoney United at the time and the approach came out of the blue. Initially, I was a bit reluctant. I'd had a very modest education and I worried that my grammar wasn't the best – I still worry about that! Though wouldn't the world be a very boring place if everybody's grammar was perfect. Eventually, I agreed to give it a go and, in time, the column grew in popularity and Lyle increased the space the paper gave to it.

I had been writing for the *Ballymoney Times* for about two years when I received an unexpected call from the Belfast *News Letter* sports editor Richard Mulligan. Richard said he wanted me to consider writing a weekly football column for the paper. At the time, I wasn't convinced that this was for me, but Richard gave me some time to think it over. When we spoke again a few days later, he explained that he had most sports covered: former Ireland rugby star Willie Anderson was on rugby; golf star Michael Hoey covered golf; world champion boxer Carl Frampton did boxing; Kyle White wrote about motorcycling; Alex Mills did the bowls section; and Denise Watson covered netball and hockey. However, he was looking for someone to cover football and he said he liked my style – he wanted someone who would shoot from the hip and tell it as it is. I liked Richard's style too and agreed to give it a go.

Back then, my computer skills were practically nil. In fact, they're still not much better today. Richard asked me if I would email my column to him. I told him I didn't do computers but that I would write the column longhand and fax it to him. The silence at the other end of the phone was deafening. Then he said, 'Liam, it's a long time since we've used fax machines. It's all done by computer nowadays but leave it with me.' A few hours later I got a call from the *News Letter* to tell me they had unearthed a fax machine in their Portadown office that they were going to clean up and I would be able to fax my column in after all.

The system worked reasonably well but the print quality of a fax is never great and between that and the fact that my text had to be retyped, it was easy for errors to creep in, which didn't please me. I knew I would have to learn how to use a computer. My kids bought me one and, since they are all competent computer users, they taught me how to use it. I don't mind admitting I made a bollocks of my early attempts and got pretty frustrated: I could only type with one finger and I agonised about even pressing the buttons. But Richard and the *News Letter* team were always helpful and understanding, and I liked working with them, even though I'm sure I caused them a few headaches. It's my style to call a spade a spade, and I won't change that ever, so Richard used to go through my column word by word to make sure that I hadn't overstepped the mark, legally or otherwise. Very often I had. Libel is a scary word in the newspaper industry, and I know that keeping me in check was a bit of a nightmare – and, on at least one occasion, I think there was some legal wrangling. But I always wanted to tell the truth as I saw it. What's the point in writing nice things about everyone when they aren't true? What's the point in just writing what you think other people would like to read or hear? That's not me and never will be. Thankfully, though, with help from Richard and his staff, I managed to deliver a weekly football column that for nine years seemed to strike a chord with readers.

Then one day in 2016, completely out of the blue, I got a phone call from Paul Ferguson, sports editor for the *Sunday Life*. He quickly laid his cards on the table: 'Liam, I have the best sports columnists in the country, and I want you for my football section.' The *Sunday Life* had been, and still is, my favourite Sunday newspaper, with the most comprehensive sports coverage in the country, so I was shocked, but nevertheless extremely pleased, to get the call and I told Paul that I was interested. But I knew that, before I accepted any offer, I wanted to do the decent thing and talk to the *News Letter*, to Richard in particular, and let them know I was speaking with the *Sunday Life* with a view to moving.

I had known Paul beforehand, though not very well, and I was pleased when he agreed that that was the best way to conduct proceedings: he wanted everything done above board as well. He explained that the role with the *Sunday Life* would be slightly different from that with the *News Letter* – that although my principal sport would still be football, he would welcome comments on all sports and sporting issues, and that I could choose how my page was set up. I could, for instance, write four short pieces or one big piece, if I wanted to. He also said that the column would run for the entire year, not just for football season. All of this really appealed to me: I was happy to write all year round; I had views on other sports and I was happy to share them. Paul gave me a few days to think it over.

My first call was to Richard at the *News Letter* and it was a tough one. He and the *News Letter* team had always been kind to me, had helped steer me away from possible High Court showdowns with the high-profile people I sometimes took to task, and I know he would have liked me to stay. But I think that, even then, my mind was made up. I was impressed by all that Paul had to say – he's a good lad who also tells it like it is – and in the end, I decided to accept his offer. I suppose I was ready to move on – the timing just felt right. Richard and I are still good friends and I'll always appreciate the fact that he gave me my start at the *News Letter*.

I've been with the *Sunday Life* for a few years now and every promise they made they've kept. Paul, too, has been incredibly supportive – he is a top-notch journalist and has been a rock, especially when, every now and again, I have overstepped the mark in my criticism of others. We have an excellent working relationship.

I really enjoy writing my column – you've got to enjoy it and relish the challenge otherwise you won't give your best – and I am fortunate that, as soon as the football season ends, the motorcycle road race season starts, which means I get to talk about sport all year round. Apparently, the page pulls in a lot of readers and, hand on heart, I find it surprising when people stop me in the street or send me messages to tell me how much they enjoy my column. With just a secondary school education I'd never harboured any thoughts that one day I'd have a full page in Northern Ireland's top Sunday national newspaper. I'm always pleased to hear that people appreciate my forthright views and comments, though I know it isn't possible to please everyone all of the time – that's the nature of the beast. But isn't that the point, to get a healthy debate going? Constructive criticism should scare no one, myself included, and while the *Sunday Life* continues to give me the freedom to write what I feel and believe, then I will always give it my best, and continue to express my thoughts on those who may try to co-opt, or indeed corrupt, sport for their own personal benefit. I'd like to give you examples but it's too risky!

It never ceases to amaze me how so many people manage to influence our sport's major decision-makers and it's something that genuinely annoys me. I'm on the record in my column for tackling issues in sport such as weak administration, loss of potential revenue through a combination of incompetence and carelessness, decisions that are driven by personal motives rather than the good of sport more generally. However, we do have some excellent and decent people who do what is right for the betterment of sport and I will always give them due praise. But as for the others, as long as I have a pen, they'll get the kick up the arse they deserve. I pander to no one.

Black Santa

In 2008, I did my first stint as Ballymoney's Black Santa – a two-week sit-out in the town centre to raise funds for charity. It all started when we were trying to raise money to erect a bronze sculpture of Robert Dunlop in the memorial garden built by Ballymoney council. Someone suggested that I become Ballymoney's first-ever Black Santa and that, as well as helping raise funds for Robert's sculpture, we would share the proceeds raised between other local charities. To be honest, I was quite reluctant at first – I knew that sitting out in the freezing cold for a solid week would be demanding, but I also knew that if we wanted a sculpture of Robert then we all had to do our bit.

I sat out in the Diamond in the town centre for a week that first year – now I do twelve days – from eight or nine in the morning until six at night, and even later when there was late-night opening for the shops and good footfall. We had a great plan in that first year that I'd be in disguise, wearing a Santa outfit and a big grey beard, and that we'd run a competition for people to guess who I was. By 9.10 on the first day, I'd been rumbled, so had to abandon that, which pleased me no end – the beard was itching the face off me.

Apart from that minor hiccup my first Black Santa was a big success and the money raised really helped us on our way towards getting the sculpture – it was finally unveiled in 2011. But as far as the Black Santa sit-out was concerned, that was it for me – I regarded that year as a one-off. However, when I saw just how the proceeds from my 2008 sit-out benefitted the local charities, I felt my resolve start to crumble. When I was asked by Ballymoney Council in 2009 if I would consider doing it again, only this time with all the proceeds being equally divided between local charities, I couldn't say no. And that was me, well and truly hooked. I have done it every year since.

Admittedly, the weather conditions can be bitterly cold or extremely wet and windy when I'm sitting out, and I have no form of heating whatsoever, but I have a little tarpaulin-type gazebo where I can shelter if the weather gets too rough. I now use foot-warmer pads that I stick to the soles of my feet before I put on my socks – they definitely help my toes, which are always like ice even on a half-decent day – and hand warmers, which I put inside my mitts. They're great too, although I continually have to take my glove off to shake hands with people – my mum was a stickler for good manners and she always told me it was bad manners not to take your glove off when you're shaking hands.

I've loads of great memories from my charity sit-outs but one that stands out happened during the dreadfully cold winter of 2010, when temperatures plummeted to minus eighteen degrees at times. Ballymoney centre was snow laden and frozen solid. In fact, one morning a good friend of mine, Robin Taggart, literally skied past me through the town centre like a slalom skier from the winter Olympics. It was like a Christmas postcard, but it was bloody freezing.

The centre was almost deserted that day because of the weather and my trousers and clothes began to freeze, so that they felt like cardboard. It was then that a lovely lady from the town – the wife of our local vet – came over to me and said, 'My goodness, Liam, you're purple with the cold and you're frozen solid. Go home and get into a hot bath.'

She was right, I was frozen solid. My lips were so cold that it was difficult to answer her. I remember saying in a slurred fashion, 'It's okay, thanks, I'll stick it out.' Off she went but was back again in no time clutching a hot-water bottle, one of the furry ones, from the local Dunnes Stores. She placed it on my knees and said, 'There Liam, hopefully that'll keep you warm.' I thanked her very much and off she went. It was so kind of her. But sadly, one vital ingredient was missing – hot water. I'd been too embarrassed to tell her, so I'd just forced a smile and let on everything was okay. At least it looked warm.

About two hours later the same lady came back in a complete fluster, 'Aw, Liam, what am I like? I left you a hot-water bottle and completely forgot to fill it with bloody hot water!' She lifted the bottle and off she went, returning a few minutes later with it full of piping-hot water. Oh boy, was I glad to see it. God love her for helping me to see that day out.

One other year I had a lady stop to ask if I could give her the money for a new washing machine as her other one had just packed in. She was deadly serious and found it difficult to understand that any money I collected went directly to local charities and that it was their decision how exactly the money would be used. She wasn't too amused when she left empty-handed.

It's a humbling experience, the Black Santa sit-out, and it never fails to restore my faith in humanity. My donations come from the rich, and the poor; from near and far and from every walk of life. For the last few years, a young schoolboy, Cain – who is getting big now – brings me a biscuit tin full of loose change that he keeps out of his pocket money every week and saves up to give me.

The five charities I donate to are the Samaritans, for whom I have been an ambassador for ten years; the Drop Inn Ministries, an organisation that brings humanitarian aid to regions across the world; St Vincent de Paul; the Salvation Army; and Compass Advocacy Network (Can), a local charity for people with learning disabilities and of which I am a patron. I've seen first-hand the tremendous voluntary work these charities do in communities and it makes me realise that I get the easy job each year. I only sit out for a couple of weeks, but the magnificent volunteers from these charities work the whole year round.

Although the Black Santa appeal is a focus for me, I am busy with charity work all year. As part of my role as an ambassador for the Samaritans I often visit Magilligan Prison in County Londonderry, where my job is to hand out awards to prisoners who have become 'Listeners', the prison equivalent of Samaritans – they try and help other inmates, particularly those who suffer from depression or mental health issues, or who may have suicidal tendencies.

Some prisoners are in for serious offences – sometimes serving life sentences – and some are in for shorter periods but continue with their voluntary work after they leave the prison. The Samaritans do tremendous work both inside the prison and outside, and it's a great honour to be associated with them.

I also have strong connections with Drop Inn Ministries, who do fantastic work both locally and abroad. In January 2019, I travelled with a Drop Inn group to Burkina Faso in Africa to unveil a freshwater drinking well for a small village out in the bush. I'd had links with the Burkina Faso area for a number of years as the proceeds that went to Drop Inn Ministries from my Black Santa work were often sent to the region. Over the years, I'd done a few additional things on my own, outside of Black Santa, to support the people there, such as sending out football kits and footballs, and so on.

In 2018, I'd been made aware that the money from my Black Santa work over the previous few years was approaching the amount needed to sink the well. My main contact at Drop Inn Ministries, Edwina Chambers, had explained to me that the kids in this village had to walk eight miles every morning with two one-gallon jars tied around their shoulders just to get fresh drinking water. I really pushed with the fundraising and, thanks to the generosity of many people, we hit the target. The money was used to employ a firm of contractors to sink the well and tap into a fresh water vein suitable for human consumption. It was quite overwhelming when I was told that the village was going to call it 'Liam's Well' in my honour, and that Drop Inn Ministries wanted me to be there for the official launch.

I was delighted to be able to go, but I did have a few concerns. I knew I'd be travelling with a group of devoted Christians and, while I believe in the Man Above, I'm still more than capable of letting slip a few swearwords now and again. I decided that the best way to deal with this was to tackle it head on. So, as we were waiting to board the plane, I took the bull by the horns and made a bit of announcement: 'I admire you all and your devotion to the Lord,' I told them, 'but I would like you to know that I'm not Christian. I don't think I'm a bad person but I'm certainly not worthy of being a Christian. And I do swear now and again. I'm not proud of it but it does happen. As long as everyone knows that.'

Of course, they couldn't have been nicer and I mostly managed pretty well when we were away. To the best of my knowledge, I only swore once. And I didn't really let myself down, except at mealtimes when I sometimes jumped the gun before Grace, which was a bit embarrassing.

Before going, I was also very concerned about the food,

as I am when I go to any foreign country. I am a very plain eater, so I knew I needed to try and bring some of my own provisions with me. I took a whole load of individual packs of porridge with me and I pretty much lived on those. Though, don't misunderstand me, the African people treated us very well. The reception we got when we arrived was overwhelming. It seemed as though all 1,100 people from the village had turned out to welcome us. They were cheering and singing, and they gave me the honour of taking the first drink of water from the well. There was a bit of money left over after the well had been built and we'd agreed to use it to provide a feast for the people of the village. They bought three cows with the money and that provided enough meat for everyone. It was quite a night, but I stuck with my porridge.

I was in Africa for ten days altogether, and during that time, we also visited several schools and orphanages, where we handed out clothes, school stationery – including pens and pencils – and some footballs. I don't think I ever have or ever will again be so moved or emotionally drained as I was by my time there. We take so much for granted, and we are all guilty of complaining over the smallest of things yet the vast majority of people I met on my trip, particularly in the bush around Burkina Faso, had little more than the clothes (or rags) on their backs. Yet they never complained and always greeted me with a smile. It was so humbling.

When we were leaving, the whole village turned out again and I had a lump in my throat. I was so conscious of how much I had compared to how little they had, and I was determined to try to do more to help. Before I'd left home, I'd been well warned by friends who had been to Africa to do charity work that I would find it emotional and that, if I went once, I would feel the need to go back. They were absolutely right. I already have plans to return early in 2020 to sink a well in another village on the outskirts of Burkina Faso. A solid group of friends are helping me with my fundraising efforts and to organise events that will generate enough money. We're hopeful that, combined with my Black Santa contribution, we will hit the amount needed.

I sometimes think of standing down as Ballymoney's Black Santa, of handing the reins over to someone else, but when I see how much help the money raised can bring to people in need, I am reluctant to walk away. And for the past couple of years I've had help – at the end of every day that I sit out, two or more members of the Ballymoney Rotary Club come and collect the day's takings and bank them. They have set up a bank account for Black Santa and they take care of all the admin, which takes the pressure off me. I couldn't manage without them now.

So, for the foreseeable future, you'll find me in Ballymoney town centre in the middle of December, wrapped up in my thermals and all the other warm clothing I can get my hands on. Even though it can be tough at times, there's a lot to be said for doing something positive. I'm happy to be doing my bit – it keeps me going.

The Palace

I'm very lucky in that I get quite a few invites to various functions and lunches/dinners throughout the year. Some of the invitations arrive via a phone call, some come in the form of a text or an email, and some come in the post. One day I was out mowing the grass at home in Ballymoney when my phone went. It was a woman from the Causeway Coast and Glens Borough Council who said, 'Liam, did you receive a very important invite in the post from us a number of weeks ago?' – I vaguely remembered a council invite to a lunch somewhere, but I'd only glanced at it and stuck the envelope behind the clock on the mantelpiece.

'May I suggest you stop mowing the lawn immediately,' the woman continued, 'and go in and read that invite properly. It's an invitation to lunch with a very important guest and the deadline for your reply is today.'

'How important is the guest?' I asked her. 'Who is it?'

'Liam, it's the Queen and Prince Philip,' she said, and I don't mind admitting I almost fell into the mower with shock.

I confirmed that I would attend immediately. To be honest, I am never too fazed about meeting important people as they eat and go to the toilet just like the rest of us, but this was the Queen, and I knew it was an honour to be chosen to meet and dine with her and Prince Philip.

The lunch was held in June 2016 at the Royal Portrush Golf Club, but I had to report to Causeway Coast and Glens headquarters at Cloonavin House, Coleraine, that morning for a security and protocol meeting. Then I was chauffeured to Portrush for the royal lunch. The security, both at the council offices and then at the golf club, was incredible, with special CCTV and security personnel everywhere. If the curtains moved, you could be mighty sure there was a James Bond-type character behind them talking into his watch. Honestly, it was mind-boggling.

It was a superb day. I was done up in my Sunday best and

both the Queen and Prince Philip were lovely people. We all met upstairs in the golf club for the formal meet-and-greet and then made our way to the dining room, where no one started eating until Her Majesty took her first bite of the spuds. She was sitting at the table just to my right and seemed pretty normal, just like the rest of us. After lunch she got up and said a few words and then it was time for us all to go our separate ways. Just so you know, you don't speak to the Queen unless she speaks to you first, and there are strictly no pictures or selfies.

After that incident, when lack of attention had almost caused me to miss out on a once-in-a-lifetime event, I made sure to look at my post more carefully. So, in 2017, when a very posh envelope dropped in through my letterbox in Ballymoney, I realised immediately it was something special. It was made of very heavy paper and it had the Buckingham Palace stamp on it. Initially, I wondered if it was one of my friends trying to stitch me up, but once I read the letter inside, I was sure this was no practical joke. This was for real. It said 'Cabinet Office' at the top and began, 'Dear Sir, The Prime Minister' – who was then Theresa May – 'has asked me to inform you, in strict confidence, that having accepted the advice of the Head of the Civil Service and the Main Honours Committee, she proposes to submit your name to the Queen. She is recommending that Her Majesty may be graciously pleased to approve that you be appointed a Member of the Order of the British Empire (MBE) in the New Year 2018 Honours List.'

I don't mind admitting I was numb and the more I read, the more numb I became. The letter was dated 20 November 2017 but it clearly stated that I wasn't allowed to tell anyone about the award until 30 December 2017, when the news embargo was lifted. But who in their right mind could get news like that and not even tell close family? Not me. My mother had been a massive fan of the royal family – there was usually a photograph of the Queen somewhere in our house, often on the mantelpiece – and my brother Lawrence and I had a real laugh at what she would have said if I'd told her I was on the Queen's New Year's Honours List, but that she wasn't allowed to tell anyone. Not a chance. She would have been so proud, she'd have been up our street knocking every door and saying, 'Don't let on, but did you hear about our Liam?' Honestly, she would not have had taken a wink of sleep for days on end.

That's probably my biggest regret about the MBE – that my mum didn't live long enough to see it and experience the visit to the palace. She was such a fan of the royals, she'd have been better dressed than the Queen herself. I remember, when someone occasionally asked for a saucer to go with their cup of tea, she would have joked, 'Where do you think you are, Buckingham Palace?' For us, a visit to Buckingham Palace was the stuff that dreams were made of. I'm quite sure that not one other person in heaven has been able to get a word in edgeways ever since the news broke that her youngest boy Liam was for the palace.

Once the news broke, I got lots of messages of congratulations from near and far, and from people from every walk of life, but there are two in particular that stand out. The first was from Harry Gregg, a man who I cherish as a close friend. Of course, Harry was very pleased for me but, as usual, he made sure I kept both feet on the ground. 'Beckett,' he said, 'you'll be still be Beckett to me. I'm very proud of you.' That meant a lot. The second came one day as I was walking through Belfast. My phone rang, and although the call was from a private number – I normally ignore those – I answered. It was Baroness Eileen Paisley, a lady I have always held in high esteem. I'd met her a few times and, despite her high profile, I always found her to be very grounded, measured and gracious. I was touched that she made the effort and had taken the time to call me personally.

I was also very lucky in that I got a call from Ricky Aitcheson, who owns a business in Broughshane, just on the outskirts of Ballymena, that specialises in custom-made suits. Ricky offered to kit me out for the palace, and I ended up with a lovely blue checked three-piece suit, along with shirt, tie, shoes, pocket-watch, breast pocket handkerchief and cufflinks. They made sure I would be dressed to perfection. In fact, on the day, one of the palace staff even told me how much they liked my suit.

It was a bit of headache trying to work out who would accompany me to the palace – I only got an invite for me, plus two. I would need eight tickets in order to bring my kids and my wife, Gillian. I had no chance. Gillian decided she'd stay at home to watch the grandchildren and let the kids go if I could get them tickets. With some maneouvring, I managed to get five tickets for family and took my sons, Lawrence, William and Robert and my daughters, Janice and Lynsey. They were as excited as I was, perhaps even more so.

The Honours ceremony was in the morning so we

decided to go over the day before and stay in a hotel close to the palace, to minimise any issues or stress on the day. We did a bit of shopping, then had a nice meal and a beer on London's famous Oxford Street.

I had no nerves whatsoever on the morning of the ceremony – I suppose that, because it was an early start, I was just too busy getting ready to worry about the day that lay ahead. The kids and I met in the hotel lobby and took a taxi to the palace – the weather was so bad that day, with dreadful snow and ice everywhere, we'd decided not to walk the short distance as we didn't want to arrive wet and frozen.

When we got to the palace gates, it started to sink in for me just how important this day was for us all and as I looked around at my children beside me, I had a lump in my throat. I was immensely proud. But there was no time for emotion as we were all rigorously security checked and then escorted in through the front entrance of the palace and into the massive foyer, which was busy with palace staff and guards. My youngest son, Robert, had me in fits when he whispered in my ear, 'Dad, are those soldiers real?' and he wasn't joking! They were absolutely motionless – they never even blinked.

After some time, the kids were taken off in one direction and I was taken off in another. But just as I was being allocated a safety-deposit box for my phone and so on, Robert appeared beside me and said, 'Will I leave my stuff here as well, Dad?' He had somehow followed me to the wrong area and cloakroom in the palace. I could do nothing but laugh and I couldn't believe he'd managed to get so far without being stopped. Only Robert could have got it so wrong. It gave us all a good laugh and relieved a bit of the tension on the day. Eventually we got him rerouted back to the rest of the family.

You never know which one of the Royal family will present your honour until you're at the palace and get to the large reception room, and the kids, especially my daughters, were hoping that William or Harry would be the ones to do it. Since I had already met the Queen and Prince Philip, I was pretty much hoping the same. So when I got to the reception room – where, again, everyone was instructed on the Royal protocol with military precision – I was pleased to find out that Prince William would be doing the honours. I knew the kids would be overjoyed. There were large screens dotted around the room, and I could see the kids on one of them. They were sitting in the second row of the family seating area and had a great view of the entire ceremony – I couldn't have been happier.

The recipients were taken in groups of about eight at a time, led out of the main holding area and through some incredibly grand corridors towards the main arena, though we were stopped several times on the way while staff name-checked everyone in the group. I could hear music playing – there was an ensemble seated at the rear of the massive hall providing the music for the ceremony. Then, when I turned that last corner and saw the immense and grand setting and Prince William surrounded by palace staff, plus all the recipients' families and friends, the penny really dropped for me. I remember thinking, 'This is it, LB. This is for real.' I felt a whole mix of emotions: immense pride for my family and friends; slight apprehension; and, as I took stock of the magnificent grandeur of the palace, I couldn't help thinking back to my youth and those days when we had nothing. Those memories are great for keeping you grounded at times like that, and I'll never forget those early years when life was a real struggle for us as a one-parent family.

However, I followed protocol to the letter. I even had time for a brief chat with a member of the palace staff while I waited for my name to be called. He whispered to me, 'William Beckett, isn't it?' 'Correct,' I said. 'It's pretty cold in here.' He replied, 'Yes indeed, sir. That's the single glazing for you, and some of the radiators don't work.' Just shows you that nowhere is perfect – even Buckingham Palace! A minute or two later, a loud voice announced, 'William Beckett MBE, for services to sport and the voluntary sector.' That was my cue, so I walked in exactly as instructed, straight ahead and then turned left to walk directly towards Prince William. There was a slight step against which your toes should rest and that's how you know it's time to stop. Prince William attached the MBE to a pre-fixed clip on my left lapel and we had a bit of a chat. He talked about football and the bikes – he had clearly done some preparation and I remember thinking, fair play to him. He's a lovely, pleasant lad who likes a laugh, and we had one. Then it was time to reverse, turn right and exit the main hall where some palace aides were waiting to remove my MBE from my lapel and put it into a presentation box for the video and pictures that were going to be taken in the palace courtyard. I was reunited with my family and they were all quite emotional. Some pictures were taken by the palace's official photographers. And that was it.

Well, not quite. We had one more treat left. Our MP, Ian

Paisley, had organised a tour of the Houses of Parliament for us immediately after we left the palace, which was a wonderful way to round off one of the most magical days of my life.

There's no place like home

I was born and reared in Northern Ireland and am immensely proud of our wee country. Despite our history of sectarianism and conflict and the wrangling of politicians, most of its people are the salt of the earth.

My sporting career has taken me all around the world, and I've seen and experienced some wonderful countries and cultures, but I could never live anywhere else. I'm always keen to get back to the 'green, green grass of home'. I love that first view of the landscape and the city as the plane comes in to land in Belfast – I know then I'm almost home. I'll be looking forward to a good builder's brew, a good Northern Ireland spud and a home-baked soda farl.

However, I don't need reminding that Northern Ireland is a fairly complex place. I was just a young man during the seventies, and I experienced the worst of our Troubles first-hand. From I was seven until I was seventeen, I lived at 31 Gate End, Ballymoney, which was virtually beside the local chapel and the adjoining Our Lady of Lourdes school. I had to pass both buildings several times a day to get to the town centre or to get to my school and the football pitches. I can remember that, as a schoolkid, when I met kids from the local Catholic school, either they crossed the road or I did, rather than pass close to one another. I stared straight ahead and so did they. How crazy was that? It was like they or I had some sort of contagious disease. It wasn't even a dislike as such, it was more something I had been brought up on – a diet of sectarianism. Not one given to me by my family, but something that came from other adults who were already 'dug in' as far as their religious and sectarian beliefs were concerned.

I remember getting involved in the odd, pre-arranged bare-knuckle fight with one of the Catholic fellas from Our Lady of Lourdes school. These scraps were always watched by a fairly large crowd of supporters from both sides – it was as much about getting the bragging rights as it was about the victory. There was no love lost between me and those other lads and it was all motivated by sectarianism. It was so wrong.

The toughest scrap I ever had was against a lad called Stewarty 'Stu' Cuddy. He was one tough and fearless guy and the fight must have lasted the best part of an hour, with both of us stubborn and unwilling to give in. The bout was finally declared a draw and we became good friends in later years. It was never in my nature to dislike other people simply because of their religion. In fact, I was pretty uncomfortable at the very thought of it, but it was the done thing back in the day and I went along with it. To be honest, I'm pretty embarrassed nowadays when I think about these things. I was probably just like most kids – I believed all I was told. I was totally gullible and vulnerable.

I am in no doubt whatsoever that my involvement in sport was a massive help in keeping me out of trouble. Back in the seventies when the Troubles were at their worst, it would have been so easy to get involved in paramilitary activities. Some of my friends did. But I was so busy with sport that that kind of thing never entered my mind. I'll be forever grateful to sport for keeping me on the straight and narrow. And I know that it's the same story for a lot of people – it's no secret that sport offers people a sense of purpose and positivity and has been the saving of young people in all kinds of contexts.

Sport has often been the glue that has kept our two communities together. It has built more bridges in our wee country than all of our politicians. Had it not have been for football and my transfer to Drogheda, I would never have crossed the border into the Republic of Ireland. The idea of doing that, especially at the height of the Troubles, would have been unthinkable to me. But playing for Drogheda changed all that. I got on great with all of the players – whether Catholic or Protestant, from the Republic of Ireland or Northern Ireland, none of that mattered. No one treated me any differently because I was a Protestant. We were all the same – we loved the game. That was a lesson that was well worth learning and it opened my mind.

In the dark days of the Troubles and beyond, sport grabbed us global headlines for all the right reasons. Dame Mary Peters, Harry Gregg, George Best, Pat Jennings, Willie John McBride, Peter Canavan, Joey Dunlop, Robert Dunlop, Phillip McCallen, Rory McIlroy, Graeme McDowell, Barry McGuigan, Carl Frampton, Dave 'Boy' McAuley and Jonathan Rea are just some of the people who reminded us and showed the world that there was a lot more to Northern Ireland than bombs and bullets.

It's because of my own experiences that I encourage young people to get involved in sport in some capacity. Yes, it's vital for their health, but it can also broaden their horizons, giving them a better understanding of other people and cultures. Through sport kids will meet and form friendships with people from all walks of life, people that perhaps they would be unlikely to meet in normal circumstances. Cross-community connections are essential if we want a humane and generous society here, and I believe that one of the best forms of cross-community interaction comes through sport.

My own children have all been keen sports people. When they were kids, I took them to the park for football and to the pool for their swimming. I was usually on the sidelines at their hockey, football and netball matches. I'm hopeful that my grandchildren will have inherited those sporting genes, and with nine of them, there's a good chance that some of them have. They're young yet, but already they're showing a big interest in swimming and football. There's always a ball lying around our house or out in the garden, and we'll usually have a kickabout at some point. They will all find their own levels and that's fine by me – I'd never want to be one of those pushy parents or grandparents that sucks all the enjoyment out of things. The taking part, the competing, the camaraderie, the friendships and, above all, the enjoyment that they will experience through sport, and will share with people from all religions and walks of life, will stand them in good stead for the rest of their lives.

My grandchildren are one of the great joys of my life. I'm lucky that most of them live nearby and there's never a day that passes without one or other of their wee faces appearing at the door. I spend far more time with them than I ever did with my own weans, and I know that's true for a lot of men of my generation. I suppose when my own kids were growing up, I was busy working and trying to provide for them, and I missed out on a lot. But you can't change what's past. So, now, I spend as much time with my kids as I can, and I make the most of my grandkids. I love a laugh and I'm guaranteed plenty of those when I'm with them. Some of the things they come out with have me doubled with laughter. Like the day I was babysitting my granddaughter Anna. She was staring at my bald head and, after a few minutes she asked, 'Grandpop, where did your hair go? Did the wind blow it off?' I was in fits of laughter, especially when she followed with, 'I don't like the wind, bad wind.' Then there was the time my wee grandson Bobby asked me why I had an extra eyebrow on my upper lip – that had me in hysterics.

I feel enormously grateful that my grandchildren are having the childhood that kids should have – the peaceful childhood that I never had. I don't want them to grow up in the divided and sectarian society that I knew, and the thought of the possible return of the paramilitaries and violence sends a shiver up my spine. But Northern Ireland has been without an assembly since January 2017, and the political impasse has left a dangerous vacuum. We urgently need the restoration of the Stormont Assembly. Our health service is on its knees and it's the same story with education. Some primary schools can hardly afford to switch on the central heating – and I've seen that first hand because I'm visiting schools on a weekly basis. Then there is sport, which is crying out for major investment.

When I look to the future, there is a lot to be positive about. Northern Ireland has so much to be proud of and so much potential, if only the political parties find enough common ground and get back to work. Otherwise, it looks like I'll have to bring my boots out of retirement, dust them down, and give all those politicians a good boot up the hole!

Acknowledgements

A very big thank you to local photographer Stephen Hamilton who took the photo that is on the front cover and to everyone who helped with pictures. Thanks too to all my family and friends and to all at Blackstaff Press, in particular my editor Patsy Horton for her expertise and endless cups of tea. Finally, I am very grateful to the one and only Harry Gregg for his foreword to my book. Harry has been my friend and inspiration for many years and I hold him and his family in such high esteem.